Front cover photo: Performer, Bali, Indonesia (credit: author)

"O eyes! O eyes! As if in one look you would
compress your whole form"
Friedrich Ruckert

Back cover photo: "The water sits", Scottish Highlands (credit: author)

"Covid-19 has upended our world and introduced an unprecedented measure of disorientation in our lives. Drawing on a wide variety of sources, Vivek Bammi's Joy Quotient *calls for the cultivation of the cosmic mind, and a reintroduction of joy, that transformative element, into daily life as we seek to rebuild from the shock of Covid and the ongoing existential threat of climate change. A fitting book for our challenging times."*

Dr. Shashi Tharoor
International author and
former United Nations diplomat

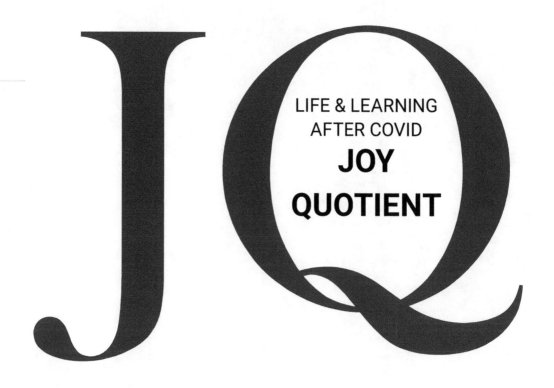

LIFE & LEARNING
AFTER COVID

JOY

QUOTIENT

Dr. VIVEK BAMMI

Cover photo: Performer, Bali, Indonesia (credit: author)

Copyright © 2021 by Dr. Vivek Bammi

ISBNs:
Paperback: 978-1-80227-176-8
eBook: 978-1-80227-177-5

Dedication

Dedicated with love and affection to:

My grandparents, for wisdom and integrity

My parents, for the gifts of a joyful childhood and independent thinking

My sons, Vihan and Veer, and my sister, Mini, for friendship and deep bonds

Bobo and Frank, for generous hospitality, conversation, and laughter

Manjula and Stuart, my soul sister and buddy

Jen Olmsted, the most gorgeous and joyful person I've come across

Southie, Harsh, Nikhil, Amita and Ted, buddies for life

My students, for the beautiful exchange of thoughts and souls

The people of Indonesia, for your civility, warmth, and beauty in gifting me a second home

Beethoven and the Buddha, for turning my life inside-out and outside-in, my eternal heroes

"Joy is rarer, more difficult and more beautiful than sadness — embrace it as a moral obligation".

Andre Gide

"If you have no relationship with the living things on this earth, you may lose whatever relationship you have with humanity".

J. Krishnamurti

"Abundance has liberated us, but not fulfilled us".

Daniel H. Pink

"I don't divide the world into the weak and the strong or the successes and the failures. I divide the world into the learners and non-learners".

Benjamin Barber

"What we really learn from a life in science is the vastness of our ignorance".

David Eagleman

"Freedom comes from dancing with the changes in life".

Jack Kornfield

"We human beings are gregarious, we are not programmed for solitude, but to give and receive".

Isabel Allende

"A fundamental concern for others in our individual and community lives would go a long way in making the world the better place we so passionately dreamt of."

Nelson Mandela

"Spontaneity, the hallmark of childhood, is well worth cultivating to counteract the rigidity that may otherwise set in as we grow older".

Gail Sheehy

"True creativity consists of gradually shedding the veiling layers of our ignorance and ego-centeredness so as to uncover the ultimate nature of both mind and phenomena".

Matthieu Ricard

"Instead of slowing down, you have to speed up".

Jane Goodall

"The last 30 years should not be the medicine years, but the magnificent years".

Norman Lazarus

"The word 'listen' contains the same letters as the word 'silent'".

Alfred Brendel

Table of Contents

Preface

As an international educator, it has been a privilege to interact with inspiring colleagues and spirited, inquiring young adults from diverse corners of the world, nurturing a pleasurable and fulfilling vocation. Nothing is more delightful than to see the boundaries and walls that often divide humans dissolve in the animated cauldron of the classroom, the playing field, the theatre, the laboratories of learning. Yet, I often sensed a missing element in the midst of these remarkable experiences, **an incomplete expansion of the mind**. The obvious constraints of "standards" and examination systems could partly explain the constriction, as well as the practical orientation of career-based schooling. However, there seemed to me to be an anomaly in the pedagogy adopted, suggesting the need for a novel and contrasting approach.

The devastation of the Covid-19 pandemic adds a sense of urgency and relevance to the search for a new paradigm of learning. The "*Qi*" or universal energy of the earth seems off kilter, our survival and wellbeing in peril. Both physical and mental health face mounting challenges, mocking the stunning extension of the human lifespan in the last century. One of my favourite film makers, Ingmar Bergman, presciently warned fifty years ago that he had "a strong impression our world is about to go under" and alarmingly, "the tragic thing is that, we neither can nor want to, nor have the strength to alter course". The outcome, he predicted, is that "an insect world is waiting for us – and one day it's going to roll in over our ultra-individualized existence"[1]. It was a virus, rather than the

---

[1] Source: Bjorkman, Stig, Torsten Manns, Jonas Sima. 1973. *Bergman on Bergman*. New York, Simon and Schuster; page 18.

"insect world", that laid us low, but his point about our lack of connectedness with other life forms was uncannily on target. Will this sobering ordeal arouse our inventive and adaptable spirit, "the strength to alter course"? **My response is firmly affirmative**, given the human capacity to learn (and unlearn) that I have witnessed in numerous settings. The "reset", though, relies upon a commitment from mentors, policy makers, thought leaders, innovators and, ultimately, each one of us. This must be a collective effort, to blunt the atomization that Bergman perceived.

We need to restore our connectedness at multiple levels – to ourselves, to others, to the planet – to restore confidence and equilibrium. I would term the "missing" ingredient that gnawed at me as an educator, reinforced by the current crisis, as **JQ**, or the **"Joy Quotient"**. As the great French writer Andre Gide noted, joy can be rare and difficult when we are confronted by numerous threats. Yet, having lived through the horrors of the two World Wars and anti-colonial conflicts, Gide saw it as a "moral obligation", a restorative for the human spirit in its quest for survival and renewal. A similar imperative can empower and impel our wellbeing in the 21st century.

Joy thrives in an expansive mode, taking its cue from our dynamic and sprightly brain; our vibrant companion at all stages of life. In JQ, we delight in extending our timespan and curiosity to learn from the majesty of cosmological, natural, and geographical forces as well as the abiding achievements of human civilizations as a shared treasure, informing our understanding and action in the present and shaping the future. The interactive and integrating brain also seamlessly bridges the artificial partitions between subject areas that schooling imposes at a young age. The "joy quotient" feasts upon the discoveries of contemporary neuroscience and guidance on robust physical exertion combined with optimal nutrition, even as quantum physics and molecular biology open vistas of wonder about our universe and miraculous enhancement of our genetic blueprint. The humanities spur our understanding of the complexities of emotion and personality, celebrating imperfection as a mark of our constant desire to evolve. The arts enthral our senses and the deepest recesses of our being in a creative rapture worthy of reverence. Spiritual traditions preserve wisdom and paths to personal and collective fulfilment. As the diverse strands converge in the animated pulse of "neural harmony", we construct a quotient with limitless possibility.

As our supreme teacher, Nature gifts us the metaphors of tending, cultivation, and flowering in the witnessing of unfolding joy. Contrasting the often frenetic pace of the present, we observe an unhurried germination of each bud blossoming at its own tempo. The learning activities and insights in this book privilege "development" and "growth" as pasture, each harvest promising the seeds of further sprouting. We embark on a journey in which the process and pleasure of the voyage far outweigh any obsession with predetermined destinations or outcomes.

As with any journey, we encounter roadblocks and potholes on the way. Apart from the momentous global perils of climate change, pandemics and unhealthy lifestyles, we confront the daily trials of distraction, stress, deprivation, mental duress and unresolved conflict. Fortunately, we can turn to several sources from wisdom traditions and contemporary knowledge to clear the path to a more skilful and comfortable navigation. A recovery from sorrow and suffering spawns the joys of resilience, grit and gratitude.

As we commence and enrich our adventure, we develop **"mental maps"** as guides, carrying the footprints of our experiences, both personal and communal. Living in an era of rapid change and innovation, our maps must mirror its fluid flow. Transience and uncertainty do not appear as implacable hazards; rather the stimuli for vigorous inquiry and the exploration of effective solutions. Collaboration and cooperation, though, remain the pillars of human survival and thriving, as they have from our origins as the "social animal".

The examples used in this book are idiosyncratic, reflecting the incredible joy of my explorations of diverse cultures and timespans as an historian and anthropologist. The global perspective is maintained throughout, for in my experience that affords us the most enthralling and credible avenue to the flourishing of ourselves and the planet. My offering carries the spirit of the Buddha, *"Ehipassiko"*, experience it for yourself. This creates room for selecting personal favourites from the vast cornucopia of human achievement. Similarly, educators and individuals could blend and adapt the learning activities in each chapter to their own context.

"Joy Quotient" finds its spark in the dynamic movement of circles of energy in the body and mind, birthing a symphony that celebrates variation and unity. Each circle contributes its own distinct melody and rhythm, yet themes and motifs recur and amplify in their flowing progression. They coalesce in the passionate sounds propelling the "Joy Quotient", fostering the spacious and extended chords of the **"cosmic mind"**. None from this or succeeding generations should be deprived of the precious gift entrusted to us by our biology and the human saga, and its enchanting potential.

Author Note

Dr. Vivek Bammi is an international educator, and has taught the Humanities and Theory of Knowledge in schools in the USA, India, the Philippines, Indonesia and China. A committed globalist, his sources of joy include travel, classical music, photography, painting, film, theatre, cuisine, cricket, tennis, and good conversation. In his active engagement with the world, passion and serenity emerge as the *YinYang* hallmarks of civilization.

Other publications:

Golden Buddhism

Indonesia: A Feast for the Senses

Theory of Knowledge for the International Baccalaureate (co-author)

Angkor: Celestial Grandeur

Deep Learning: A Journey in Critical Thinking and Reflective Knowledge (co-author)

Acknowledgements

With gratitude, I would like to acknowledge the contribution of the following to the germination of the *Joy Quotient*:

My mentors at Carnegie-Mellon University, Pittsburgh, including Professors Ted Fenton, Tony Penna, Peter Stearns, Barry Beyer, Ludwig Schaefer, Donald Sutton and Dr. Bernard Ulozas.

Dr. Niall Nelson and Mr. Malcolm McKenzie, for sterling leadership.

My colleagues at Kodaikanal International School, International School Manila, Jakarta Intercultural School, and Keystone Academy Beijing, for endless stimulation, bonhomie, and upholding the nobility of our profession.

My teachers and schoolmates at the Doon School, Dehra Dun, for enduring foundations and friendship.

The Theory of Knowledge "gang of 23"– fonts of wisdom, humour, and deep humanity.

Deniek Sukarya and Arun Taneja, for sharing the joys of photography.

Professor Tracey Tokuhama-Espinosa of the Harvard University Extension School, for opening up the incredible vista of contemporary research on neuroscience and multiple fields, which I have drawn upon liberally.

Introduction

Premonitions of a crippling crisis to strike humans and our planet had been in the air since the beginning of the 21st century, with deadly diseases and catastrophic climatic events surfacing in different corners of the globe. Yet, we were caught vastly under-prepared for the devastating impact of the Covid-19 pandemic in 2020. An invisible lurking menace grounded our movement across continents, destroyed millions of livelihoods, strained our health systems, and conjured lonely deaths and grief for its victims. The greatest disruption to learning and education in living memory may have dashed the dreams of an entire generation. It cast an ominous shadow on everyone, from Presidents and Prime Ministers to ordinary citizens and the impoverished.

In many ways, Covid could be viewed as an accelerator and magnifier of trends that were already evident in the preceding decades. It laid bare the vulnerabilities of our bodies and minds in a stark manner. Despite the incredible expansion of the human lifespan in the last century, the 'pandemics' of poor health (exemplified by obesity and other forms of malnutrition coupled with sedentary lifestyles), lowered immunity, and emerging mental crises of anxiety, depression, and dementia had already crept up on us before the virus delivered a crippling blow.

The culminating impact of industrial lifestyles and Covid on physical and mental wellbeing carries the hallmarks of a *"Tsunami"*, but an even graver tidal wave threatens humanity and the planet as global warming and climate change unleash catastrophic fires and floods in different parts of the world. Rising temperatures have created a similarly bleak scenario in our polar regions: "The last fully intact ice shelf in the Canadian

Arctic has collapsed, losing more than 40% of its area in just two days at the end of July, 2020 (Warburton)". The resultant increase in sea levels could spell doom for some of our best known coastal cities, quite apart from the calamitous impact on wildlife.

These combined threats could, though, become the wake-up call that we desperately needed. Every crisis can be viewed as both a challenge and an opportunity, to regain trust in human ingenuity, resolve, and wisdom. Indian author and social commentator Arundhati Roy sees the possibilities of renewal: "historically, pandemics have forced humans to break with the past and imagine their world anew. This one is no different. It is a portal, a gateway between one world and the next. We can choose to walk through it, dragging the carcasses of our prejudice and hatred, our avarice, our data banks and dead ideas, our dead rivers and smoky skies behind us. Or we can walk through lightly, with little luggage, ready to imagine another world" (Roy).

Despite the "carcass" of a leadership crisis made evident in some countries, a positive outcome of Covid in many other nations has been the restoration of faith in scientific expertise[2] and community ties in confronting the virus. Women leaders in Germany, Taiwan, and New Zealand presented leadership models of competence and compassion that could alter the political landscape in our century. **A similar transformation must permeate our education systems, the foundations of society.** While we have made some attempt at moving beyond the "industrial model" of learning, which prioritized rote and conformity to established structures, we are some distance away from constructing the innovative, adaptable, resilient, and enlightened schooling that would assist us in confronting multiple challenges, and ensuring a positive legacy for the generations to follow.

---

[2] On a global level, we can marvel at the development of effective vaccines to control Covid infection within a year of the pandemic, a feat never achieved before in medical science.

The notions of IQ and EQ have certainly contributed some beneficial outcomes to education. Despite continuing reservations about cultural bias, IQ tests have accurately predicted success in academic settings as well as in a range of occupations. The Emotional Quotient may present some obvious obstacles in measurement, but the increasing recognition of "emotional intelligence" as an important predictor of life success, in terms of both self and social awareness, added a vital strand in our understanding of human behaviour and personality. Yet, these are clearly not adequate in addressing the physical and mental suffering underlying our existential crisis. **We need a new paradigm**, building upon some of the earlier insights and practices, but reaching toward a more expansive human connection – to Nature, to others, to the self. We must "imagine another world", in Arundhati's words.

My vision and conviction is to introduce JQ or the "Joy Quotient", so that human potential may flourish in a nurturing partnership with the forces that we have wantonly ignored or destroyed in a paroxysm of greed, hatred, and ambition. We now have the tools and capabilities to bring together understandings from the sciences, humanities, arts and wisdom traditions from all corners of the globe in a meaningful and deeply engaging synthesis.

Joy is animated by a sense of physical and mental wellbeing that ripples outward from the individual to the community, to other species and to the planet, all of whom are under threat. It is not considered a static or permanent state, rather dynamic and flowing, requiring constant renewal, attention, and application. **As a "quotient", it could only be 'measured' in its inherent infinity, mirroring the boundless vitality of our most animated organ, the brain.**

Including a series of insights and learning activities, JQ presents a blueprint for lifelong learning and exploration, a celebration of the human spirit at each stage of its cultivation and flowering,

embracing people of all ages. With the auspicious insights from science on "neuro-plasticity"[3] or the ability of the brain to adapt and evolve and construct new connections throughout the human lifecycle, we may now speak of a "**brain span**" as much as a "lifespan". We are "live wired" (Eagleman) for networking and expansion, with conscious awareness of this potential.

Although the impact from, and response to, Covid may have exemplified a retreat from "globalization" in some aspects, **it has not removed the validity of a global worldview.** As a new paradigm of learning, JQ builds upon this inclusive perspective that would restore trust in human exchange and thriving, with the hope of preventing a future cataclysm. The concepts and learning activities in this book draw liberally upon exciting observations from current scientific research in leading world universities, especially in neuroscience, nutrition and the "gut-brain axis", creativity and the arts, sports and exercise, as well as successful aging. At the same time, we delve into the wisdom of established practices of meditation, mindfulness, social and ethical learning, effective leadership, and the growth mind-set, each contributing to what the Greeks called "*eudaimonia*" or human flourishing.

The framework for this new approach is imbued with the French historian, Fernand Braudel's notion of **the three "cycles of time":** the **geological/geographic** cycles, which are shaped by millennia where change is barely perceptible, except in a disaster or catastrophe; the **historical/cultural (or civilizational)** cycles, which are shaped by centuries, and change slowly at an evolutionary pace, except in the case of revolution; and, the **current events** cycles, which are shaped by years, hours and minutes, change is palpable and the focus of most media coverage

---

3   Neuroscientist Prof. David Eagleman prefers the term "live wired" to capture the dynamic capacity of the brain to constantly reshape its circuitry; with 86 billion neurons or brain cells, each with 10,000 connections, he says its potential for change "bankrupts our language" (Eagleman).

(Braudel). The challenges posed by Covid and climate change provide an opportunity to look beyond current events and draw inspiration from the other two cycles: a clear understanding and celebration of our links with nature and the restoration of an ecological worldview, coupled with an honouring of the ingenuity of human civilizations which tackled previous threats to survival and left us a legacy of brilliance. We build generously upon the insights of indigenous cultures as much as the great civilizations that graced every continent. **Their wisdom is not viewed as simply an accumulation of knowledge, but as a lived reality that is deeply relevant to our times.**

The book draws particular inspiration from a trio: Ludwig van Beethoven, who symbolizes the passion of the Western mind in an unbroken thread from the Greeks to the quantum physicists and neuroscientists of our day; the Buddha, an icon of Eastern wisdom whose enlightened awareness reached every corner of the globe; and the goddess Sarasvati, the origin of knowledge and discernment, the feminine force without which we would not exist. In Beethoven's music we discern the spiritual evolution of a soul that encountered daunting tribulations and emerged with a triumphant vision of human possibility. The Buddha confronted the stark reality of multi-dimensional human suffering and offered a path of balanced contentment and harmony. In nature, Sarasvati takes on the form of the river, a metaphor of dynamic and eternal movement. In her Balinese embodiment, she gifts us the notion of "*Rwa Bhinneda*" or "two differences", a reminder that the ultimate truth lies beyond the grasp of human limitation, guiding us into the realm of the unknown.

Covid-19 presented us a graphic reminder of the uncertainty of our knowledge as much as life itself, leading us to question the assumptions of mathematicians, scientists, and policy makers alike. **However, rather than viewing it as a failing, we could approach uncertainty and the unknown as spurs to inquiry, creativity and exploration.** Buddhist philosopher, Jack Kornfield, refers to the teacher, Roshi Suzuki's delight in the **"beginner's mind"** as a dimension of inner freedom, and quotes the universal thinker, J. Krishnamurti: "truth is a pathless land…no one has ever lived your life before" (Kornfield). **The embracing of uncertainty opens the door to a more flexible and passionate outlook on learning, what we may call a "fluid intelligence".** With this "celebration of tentativeness" (Kornfield), we begin the journey from the "beginner's mind" toward a "cosmic mind" that embodies the glow of the Joy Quotient.

Book Structure: The Eight Circles of Joy

The book builds upon the Indian concept of the **"chakras" or cycles of energy** which permeate the physical, emotional and mental strands of human existence, arising within the body and expanding outward in our interaction with others. They are used as a scaffolding, shorn of any specific cultural association. Although more than a hundred "chakras" have been identified, there are seven prominent sources with an eighth that is intuited to hover just above the body. We may thus conceive of the **"eight circles of joy"**, each emanating its own lucid vitality while partaking of the feast of passion and vigour in constant circulation. Distinct, as well as overlapping themes or "leitmotifs", shape the symphony in coalescing chords. Each circle will introduce the audience to recommended readings, broadcasts and performances, as well as learning activities or experiences which cover the entire range from school to adult education, combining theoretical perspectives with practical application.

The first circle, located at the base of the spine, ignites the uncoiling of our energy and learning potential. Here we examine our relationship with Nature, Braudel's geographical cycle, the source of universal energy, cultivation, and sustenance. In the current context, the urgent task of confronting climate change and global warming would be an essential element of action. We build upon the impetus of curiosity and the skill of observation as the foundations for joyful and meaningful exploration. The second circle, centred at the lower abdomen, emanates in sensual energy, procreation, and fertility. The cultivation of the senses and sensory perception become the base for the intricate layering of scientific study and artistic creation, underlying the richness of our civilizations and their achievements.

At the third circle, converging at the navel, we encounter the vitality of the "second brain", informed by our understanding of the "gut-brain axis" and the vital roles of nutrition, diet and exercise in ensuring lifelong wellness. Emotionally, "gut feeling" could be the essential ingredient in launching and maintaining some of our deepest relationships, which are enhanced by the laughter and humour radiating from the belly. We may also marvel at the "navels" of civilizations, cultural and spiritual centres that inspired countless generations. The fourth circle partakes of the emotional energy orchestrated in the heart. We explore the impact of destructive and positive emotions in shaping human personality and social outcomes and cull secrets of happiness from a range of cultures. The case for social, emotional and ethical education as a crucial ingredient in contented and joyful living is considered.

The fifth circle flows from the throat in a cascade of expressive energy and excellence. That most precious gift of our biology, the voice box, articulates a celebration of poetry, song, speech and debate, enthralling, challenging and uniting humans across cultural and temporal barriers. Its elaboration in the written word adds a fertile strand of pleasure and joy in an inclusive embrace. At this stage, energy begins to merge with invisible yet potent contours. The sixth circle, initiated at the pineal gland or the "third eye", transmits the exuberance of intuitive, creative, innovative and lateral thinking, completely relevant to our restlessly inventive age. "Design" may be seen as our ruling metaphor, manifesting in the arts as much as in the sciences and technology. At the same time, established practices of meditation and mindfulness provide the necessary balance we need for judgements arising from inner awareness and clarity.

At the seventh circle, we arrive at the pinnacle, a concentrated and heightening energy of synthesis and realization united at the crown of the head and the encased brain. We are inspired here by philosophers, film-makers, and sports performers alike in their quest for the deepest understandings, portrayals of human complexity, and the striving for focused excellence. The joy at this level exudes the euphoria of a symbiosis or a "**neural harmony**". Yet, we must move beyond to the subtle and imperceptible tones of the eighth circle. Listening, the most important skill in learning, leads us into silence, disturbed only by the voice of gratitude at the abundance of delight gifted to us by the cosmic genius.

SOURCES/CITATIONS

Braudel, Fernand. 1972. *The Mediterranean and the Mediterranean World in the age of Philip II*. Fontana/Collins, London.

Eagleman, David. *"Neuroplasticity with Professors David Eagleman and Andrew Huberman"*. www.youtube.com/watch?v=zc_OXqCRL1g&t=449s. Sept. 5, 2020. Accessed 15.9.2020.

Kornfield, Jack. *"The Wisdom of Uncertainty"*. www.youtube.com/watch?v=V3torYqRaOI&t=773s. July 7, 2017. Accessed 24.10.2020.

Roy, Arundhati. *"The pandemic is a portal"*. Financial Times. April 3, 2020.

Warburton, Moira. *"Canada's Last Fully Intact Arctic Ice Shelf Collapses"*. Reuters. June 20,2020.

The First Circle of Joy

The first circle sets in motion the uncoiling of energy which will find fruition in multiple pathways to wellbeing. We pay homage to the source of universal energy, called "Qi" by the Chinese and "Prana" by the Indians, recognizing ourselves as just one of the organisms that share that vitality. That sense of connectedness to "Qi", the "relational awareness" urged by ecologist Merlin Sheldrake, is a pathway to unbounded joy at both individual and community levels. However, it is also informed by the urgent need for vigilance and a commitment to reverse the wilful destruction of other beings that we have unleashed in the last two centuries. In particular, the gathering pace of climate change, global warming and environmental devastation require changed attitudes and behaviours from each one of us.

In this circle, we hear the perspectives of a devoted naturalist and a budding environmentalist, linked by their deep concern for the renewal of the planet. An astrophysicist reminds us of the astonishing transformation of cosmic forces that enabled us to breathe and exist. A microbiologist and a forest scientist lead us into the fascinating world of underground communication of plants and how this could affect our understanding of individuality and community across species. We are inspired by the reverence for nature of some of our earliest human societies, the Australian aborigines and Native Americans, and its celebration in the arts – we have much to learn from them. The botanist with Native American ancestry, Robin Wall Kimmerer, likens the intricate tendrils of moss to "the intertwined threads of a Beethoven quartet", coupling the beauty of nature with the most profound expression of the human mind. We further rejoice in the symphony of nature and the arts in the works of Monet, Wordsworth, and Debussy. They amplify Braudel's idea of the "longue durée", uniting us with longer cycles of time, both geographical and historical.

A similar connectedness prevails in the **learning activities** in this circle. We are invited to develop a harmonious and caring relationship with our living environment, radiating from childhood years to lifelong behaviour. This flows from the evolution of our "mental map", a guide to our understanding and action in the world. The arts, especially when allied with nature, gift us boundless pleasure and we can learn from the ingenuity of others. We also revel in the joy of movement, an energizing accompaniment throughout the lifespan.

The learning activities are rooted in curiosity, observation, listening, creativity, and compassion, the blueprint for an expansive engagement with the self and with others. **They could create the cornerstone for a world-or planet-centred education** (Biesta). Nobody could serve as a greater inspiration for this endeavour than Leonardo da Vinci, the multi-faceted genius of the Italian Renaissance. As Michael Gelb puts it, we can "think of his example guiding us to be more of what we truly are" (Gelb xiii).

We begin the circle with an elegy to nature, in recognition of our destructive impact and the need for change. We end on a note of celebrating nature and our eternal ties with it. Beethoven, like da Vinci, urges us to discover the best in human possibility.

An Elegy to Nature and the Need for Renewal:

Sir David Attenborough, "Life on our Planet" (Netflix, October 12, 2020)

In a lifetime committed to passionate observation and understanding of our planet, Sir David has documented the loss of its wild places and its bio-diversity, which he calls "a finely tuned life support machine", blaming bad planning and human error. In 1937, the world's population was 2.3 billion, the carbon in the atmosphere was 280 parts per million, and the remaining wilderness was 66%; by 2020, the world's population stands at 7.8 billion, carbon is 415 parts per million, and the remaining wilderness shrunk to 35%; within a single lifetime, the global decline is apparent as humans have over-run and destroyed the non-human world. The famous "Serengeti" in East Africa means "endless plain", but in fact the wild is far from unlimited and needs our protection. From space, our planet appears vulnerable and isolated, and Sir David urges a "changed mindset" to preserve its diversity. Examples of our destruction abound: mountain gorillas in Africa decimated by poaching for their babies; industrial whaling and over-fishing depleting ocean resources and leading to "empty nets" and unravelling in the shallows with entire coral reefs turned into ghostly wastelands; the felling of half the rainforest in Borneo to replace tree diversity with oil palm monoculture, reducing the population of Orangutans by two-thirds. Our planet is losing its ice with rising recorded temperatures in almost every year of the last decade and warming Arctic summers, the oceans unable to absorb the heat from our activities and rising sea levels already impacting low lying and coastal areas.

"Our assault has finally come to alter the very fundamentals of the living world" (Attenborough), with daunting consequences for ourselves. There are predictions that by the 2030's the Amazon, our greatest store of oxygen, could turn from rainforest to dry savannah, altering the global water cycle. Global warming would lead to thawing of frozen soils, releasing more greenhouse gases like methane and contributing further to climate change. The oceans become more acidic, fish populations crash, and we could face a global food crisis. By 2100, the planet could be 4 degrees centigrade warmer, making large parts of it uninhabitable and making billions homeless. We could indeed be heading into the "sixth mass extinction".

Sir David calls for a "vision" and several concrete steps to restore the stability and diversity of the living world. Every species has a sustainable population, and humans must stop or slow our demographic surge; the urgent needs of poverty reduction, adequate health care, and education (especially for girls) emerge as priorities for 'developing' nations as well as pockets of deprivation in the 'developed'. The switch from fossil fuels to renewable and "green" energy is now a well recognized strategy in several countries, including some of the current major carbon emitters and polluters. A reduction in carbon, and creating "no-fish zones" in one-third of coastal areas could revive marine habitats as the greatest wildlife reserve. Contracting the area usurped for farming would necessitate a move toward more plant based diets, as meat production encroaches on huge expanses of land. Urban farming and sustainable family farms (as in Holland) would also reverse the "land grab". Oil palm plantations and soya cultivation could be restricted to de-forested areas to rehabilitate our forests as carbon containers. As Sir David reminds us, Nature is our biggest ally and our greatest inspiration, requiring an **attitude of mutual caring.** What is at stake is our own survival.

The Young Ornithologist: Bird Watching, Activism and an Environmental Worldview

Mya-Rose Craig, the 18-year old bird watcher and environmental activist (from an article in the London Times, October 9 2020, by Michael Odell):

A committed observer of birds since she was a young girl, the British-Bangladeshi Mya has just published her memoir, titled *Birdgirl*. She says the interest it aroused shows that "with everything that's going on in the world right now, perhaps people really are rediscovering the beauty and necessity of the natural world". She has also been called the "British Greta Thunberg" in a comparison with the Swedish teenage environmental activist. "Last month she went to the Arctic, just north of Svalbard, Norway, to take part in the most northerly 'youth climate strike' protest to date. Craig travelled there on a Greenpeace ship, then balanced on an ice floe, placard in hand…she wanted to highlight the fact that, pandemic or not, the Arctic ice is reportedly melting faster than ever".

Her primary obsession, though, remains the birds: "the excitement of seeing a species you've never seen before never leaves you". With expeditions to 38 countries over seven continents with her family, she has spotted more than 5,000 of the world's 10,738 species. The family's first trip to South America was based on research on a global bird database, *Avibase*. Mya had to confront her fear of heights and spiders, swaying on top of a 200 foot-high bird-viewing platform in Ecuador, besides encountering a species of jumping spider in Colombia that leapt as high as her waist and a tarantula in Chile. She has also had to contend with trolling after starting her *Birdgirl* blog, with some questioning the right of a young Muslim to enjoy birdwatching. "I've grown up to be tough about it", she says; "Some people think you're arrogant or misguided for speaking up about birds, the environment, and biodiversity…I've seen how Greta gets criticised, but she is amazingly strong. Like her, I really do focus on the fact that this is my generation's future at stake".

Mya helped to set up the youth organization Black2Nature, which attracts black and ethnic minority children to her weekend birdwatching camps. She says, "I try to mix up the groups so that we have some inner-city children and some local enthusiasts. A lot of the children from inner cities have never even seen a sheep before, and it's so lovely to see them get excited by nature…it seems really sad that everyone doesn't enjoy something that is so good for our mental health".

Mya-Rose Craig has turned her passion for birds into a complete worldview: "She has become a vegetarian for environmental reasons. And after a trip to Borneo during which the family drove for five hours through jungle cleared for palm oil plantations (there were no birds), she has become a fervent campaigner against palm oil overproduction". She says that "seeing what is happening to our world with your own eyes is really frightening".

For all its terrible cost, the measures to combat Covid-19 have reduced environmental pollution and helped to restore some aspects of biodiversity. As Mya says, "the great challenge is to make that recovery permanent".

Learning Activity: Constructing your "mental map" (for high school students and adults at any age):

A "mental map" represents what may be considered our "inner GPS", providing direction as we navigate the challenges and possibilities of life. It tends to be highly dynamic and malleable in the young, developing brain with greater stability in the middle and later years. However, the understanding of neural plasticity opens the door to constant reconfiguration of the map. It may be considered a "worldview", but one subject to transformation and enrichment at any stage of life.

In the case of Mya-Rose Craig, we see how her mental map and practices are being shaped by her passion for ornithology and commitment to tackle the global threat of climate change.

In this activity, every student and adult constructs their own mental map, using the format that they prefer: a "brainstorming" visual with multiple elements, a drawing, a song. We can begin to see if there is a coherence emerging in the map: in Mya-Rose's case, her decision to become vegetarian, to join a protest against global ice melt, and setting up an organization to introduce others to the wonders of nature. This coherence may not be complete, since the map is open-ended. The individual map is also influenced by others, so we may consider "community" and "cultural" mental maps as well.

This activity should be revisited at regular intervals, as we note the evolving contours of our understanding.

Australian Aboriginal Art: The "Dreamtime" and an Ecological Worldview

Dating back more than 40,000 years, the Australian aborigines represent among the oldest continuous human cultures and artistic traditions

(Hossack). As nomadic groups, much of the art was ephemeral, done on transportable materials like bark or wood, or restricted to outsiders because of its sacred nature (such as rock art). However, since the 1970's (when they were finally accepted as Australian citizens), their art has become more permanent and its striking themes and colours displayed in galleries around the world. More importantly, we recognize that **Aboriginal art expresses a profound worldview or "mental map" that carries vital significance for us today.** Much of Aboriginal art embodies the "**Dreamtime**", the genesis of life when Creation spirits set up a holistic relationship between nature, animals, and humans. These are not just documents of history and culture, but also a guide to respectful behaviour toward the land and a deep sense of belonging to it. Circles, which are prominent in the art, could represent a camp site, a fire place, water hole, sacred area or an initiation ceremony (Jones). Time is not seen as linear, but as cyclical, implying an eternal cycle of sacred law, including hunting in the right season. Song cycles celebrate rivers, trees, and food sources, while reinforcing the message of replenishing the land. Hands become symbols of identity and belonging, as well as a sign of respect for Nature and its bountiful creation. The Aborigines were and are "**natural ecologists**" (Jones), **understanding and living with a mutual caring for the land** which Attenborough sees as imperative for our times.

Learning Activity: Aboriginal Art (for all ages)

1. We first explore three art works by contemporary Aboriginal artists:

   Artist Nellie Marks Nakamarra
   Dreaming: Traveling through my country (2011)
   www.youtube.com/watch?v=504IxoTETEU&t=238s
   May 11, 2011. Accessed: 27.9.2020

   Artist Judy Watson Napangardi
   Dreaming: Mina Mina (2011)

https://www.youtube.com/watch?v=je4WxI2aIZk
February 18, 2011. Accessed: 27.9.2020

Artist Ronnie Tjampitjinpa
Dreaming: Bush Fire (2011)
https://www.youtube.com/watch?v=cK5l9zoPRYk
May 18, 2011. Accessed: 28.9.2020

2. For each art work, discuss the themes and motifs used by the artist (with your class or discussion group) and how they relate to "Dreamtime" and the creation of a culture of "natural ecologists".

3. Create your own artwork, inspired by Australian aboriginal motifs (**suitable for young students**)

https://www.youtube.com/watch?v=8RZzLEoMCQE
June 5, 2012. Accessed: 28.9.2020

In this activity, we see the value of art in introducing very young students to the diversity of animals and the use of multiple symbols in earliest human art, with the underlying themes of respect and caring for nature. Teachers in different parts of the world could tap into early art from their region, such as Adivasi art in India, rock art in Africa, and cave art in Indonesia and Europe.

Everything is Connected: Three Stories

Tom Chi- astrophysicist, technologist, inventor
https://www.youtube.com/watch?v=rPh3c8Sa37M,
TedX Taipei, January 12, 2016. Accessed 25.9.2020.

Astrophysicist Tom Chi presents three wonderful stories of "connection" that link our most intimate and vital facets to both cosmic and civilizational forces. **The first story is of the heart**. The reason that our heart is beating is because it needs to move haemoglobin, which carries a smaller molecule, an iron atom, enabling us to bind oxygen and move it through the circulatory system. The only way iron is created in the universe is through the forming and explosion of supernovas and super massive stars, which eventually enabled iron to course through our veins. Formed through galactic collisions, which set up a gravitational structure called "*Laniakea*" (Hawaiian for "immeasurable heaven"), this connects every heartbeat in our physical sphere.

The second story is of the breath, which was not possible 3 billion years ago on our planet, since there was almost no oxygen and only single celled organisms in existence. The process of forming oxygen in the atmosphere could be credited to some "cyano-bacteria" which had the capacity for photosynthesis, taking energy from the sun and transforming carbon dioxide into oxygen. The ozone layer formed 600 million years ago, and could begin to support complex multi-cellular life. With the Cambrian Explosion, we had life in the seas and plants on land, as tiny organisms formed into "chloroplasts". Our every out-breath is mirrored in the in-breath of a plant and its converse.

The third story is of the mind, and here Tom presents the tale of our relationship with the piano, which was invented around 1700 C.E. The instrument is so nuanced, textured, and carries so much beauty that people can make a career and a lifetime of playing this instrument and giving pleasure to audiences worldwide. A brain committed to this instrument must have the ability to coordinate ten fingers, to work the pedal, to convey the feeling of the sound as well as an understanding of music theory. The invention of this beautiful pattern and structure in the brain was not an independent thought; it required a depth of mechanical engineering and knowledge of the history of stringed instruments. Today, we find mastery of the piano in cultures very distant from its European roots, exemplified by pianists Lang Lang and Yuja Wang from China and Mitsuko Uchida from Japan.

Our bonds with other civilizations and experiences of humanity gift us what Tom calls the "**Palette of Being**". With our endlessly creative mind, we expand this palette, adding new colours and ways of expression. We may appear tiny and unimportant in relation to the biosphere and society, but we have the ability to shape others and the way they are able to perceive in the future. All our spiritual traditions promote this linkage, radiating outward from the individual to family and friends, society, the biosphere, and the physical universe. **The core of science contains a similar understanding of connectedness**, which is literally true for the physical universe at every level of its organization and manifestation of energy, matter, and life. We must challenge ourselves to live with this truth.

Learning Activities: Listening to the power of Water

Following from Tom Chi's story of the connection of the human mind and the piano, listen to a haunting and mesmerizing piano work by French composer Debussy (1862-1918).

Claude Debussy – La Cathedrale Engloutie ("The Engulfed Cathedral"). Piano: Nelson Freire
https://www.youtube.com/watch?v=cVMGwPDP-Yk

The piece echoes a Breton myth of a cathedral that was submerged by the sea off the island of Ys. Through the morphing tones and moods of the work we can envisage the reappearance of the cathedral, a renewed feasting of our ears on its bells and the organ, before it is engulfed again by the mighty power of water.

The piece is a beautiful rendition of the symbiosis of humans and nature, and a reminder of our relative insignificance in the cosmic drama.

One of the seminal texts of Chinese civilization, the *Dao de Jing or "The Classic of the Way and Virtue"*, similarly honours water as the central element in sustaining life as well as influencing human thought and action: "Water is explicitly described as sustaining the growth of *wan wu*, 'everything in the world', but willing to dwell at the lowest levels" (Lu). Although it appears weak and gentle, it is inexhaustible and it always returns: "Nothing in the world is as soft and weak as water and yet in attacking what is hard and strong, nothing can surpass it" (Lu). We hear this clearly in the "Engulfed Cathedral".

Flowing Water – Guan PingHu (guqin)
https://www.youtube.com/watch?v=FIYY4un8h1E
April 29, 2011. Accessed: 6.6.2021

The Chinese arts were deeply influenced by the *Dao*, which flowered in celebration of our harmony with nature in painting, poetry, and music. In this enchanting piece, Guan PingHu exalts the eternal rhythms of water on the "*guqin*", an ancient stringed instrument. This recording was included in the world music sent into outer space by the Voyager craft, an apt blend of two universal forces.

Water is the great teacher. Being adaptable and flexible, it inspires us to remain flowing in constant exploration, in reinventing ourselves, in combining humility with strength of purpose. These form the foundations for skilful thinking and agile action.

Conversations in, and with, nature:

Merlin Sheldrake – The philosophy of fungi (Conversation with Freddie Sayers of UnHerd TV):
https://www.youtube.com/watch?v=CZlmQHlZBCE
(Sept. 10, 2020; Accessed 12.9.2020)

Biologist and ecologist Merlin Sheldrake became interested in decomposition organisms which led him to a study of fungi that oversee so many of these natural transformations. It relates to the subject of symbiosis, of organisms that live together intimately and shape life on the planet, in which fungi are major players. Mushrooms and fungi form part of "mycorrhizal networks" under the ground, burrowing into wood, animal bodies, and soil; unlike most organisms, they put their bodies into the food. With efficient ways of searching space, they behaved as the root system of ancestor plants for the first 60 million years on life on land - to scavenge in the soil, find mineral networks, and exchange with plants for sugar in photosynthesis. They form part of, and mediate, a **wood-wide web**", an overlapping symbiotic network connecting organisms. It is particularly fascinating how they form new relationships and commandeer animal bodies to spread fungal spores. For example, fungi grow into ants and form chemicals that alter their behaviour, compelling them to climb up plant stalks (called "summit disease") and bite the vein of the leaf in a "death grip". Sprouting from the stalk's head, the fungus becomes a prosthetic organ on the ant's body or "fungus in ant's clothing"!

Sheldrake sees philosophical implications of this blurring of the lines between creatures for the non-fungal world, including our own. He raises questions on our notion of a "neatly bounded" individuality, pointing out that we carry more microbes than our own cells, which play a part in digesting food, preventing disease, and in influencing behaviour. In this delicate, balanced relationship with other organisms, "we are not a neatly definable biological unit" and a large part of our genome started as viruses, **Covid-19 serving as a poignant reminder of this biological reality.**

Sheldrake's training as an ecologist shapes his understanding of the dynamical systems of Nature as **"integrated wholes"** rather than as distinct parts, a viewpoint that resonates remarkably with the perspectives of the Australian aborigines as well as the naturalist, ornithologist, and astrophysicist that we looked at earlier. In understanding the multiple levels of "selfhood" and softening the boundaries of ourselves, we can re-evaluate our relationships with other forms of life. Studying micro-organisms develops humility as we recognize their presence before and after the existence of larger species.

Sheldrake also warns of the possibility of recurring and deadly pandemics if we persist with the destructive practices of de-forestation, habitat destruction, and large scale industrial farming, including the use of antibiotics in farm animals that breed new bacterial "superbugs". A different perspective, based on a **relational awareness of our symbiotic ties with other organisms**, would underlie our commitment to a sustainable ecosystem and our own preservation.

Suzanne Simard: How Trees Talk to Each Other
https://www.youtube.com/watch?v=Un2yBgIAxYs
August 30, 2016; Accessed: 24.9.2020

In a good companion piece to Sheldrake's study of micro-organisms, Suzanne Simard urges us to look at the infinite biological pathways which would enable us to think of forests as a single organism and to reverse the alarming rate of clear cutting in her area (British Columbia in Canada). Using scientific methods and instruments, Simard showed evidence of an "underground communications network" in which the Paper birch and the Douglas fir behave as exchanging and interconnected species in a "*Yinyang*" mutually reinforcing relationship. They converse in the language of carbon, nitrogen, water, phosphorus, hormones, and allele chemicals. Using a similar metaphor to Sheldrake of a dense web akin to the internet, she highlights the role of the "mycelium" or "fungal highways" in promoting the trade of carbon for nutrients in the forest. In another fascinating observation, "hub" or "mother" trees were seen to nurture their young, sending excess carbon through a network to seedlings, increasing their rate of survival. Mother trees also seem to recognize their "kin", sending more carbon to their species and reducing root competition to make elbow room for their growth. When dying, they convey their wisdom to the next generation with defence signals that would increase their resilience and resistance to future stresses.

In 2014, the World Resources Institute listed Canada as the country with the highest "forest disturbance rate" in the world, though Brazil must enter into the reckoning with the recent assault on its Amazon rainforest. Simard calls for a change in forestry practices from clear cutting and use of herbicides to holistic and sustainable methods. Among the solutions would be to maintain a diversity of species and genotypes, based on knowledge of local conditions, saving old growth forests, and greater local involvement in their conservation. With a changed attitude, we can rely on the intelligence of forests to self-heal, since the science shows us that they are "**super collaborators**".

Learning Activity: Observing Growth and Changes in Plants (primary school students)

This extended experiment was planned and conducted by my former colleague, Leah Newey, at Keystone Academy, Beijing:

1. Students select a vegetable plant and read the provided information about it. They go to the school garden and plant the correct amount of seeds in the allocated sections.

2. The class arranges all the plants in the garden bed together and maps them onto the growveg.com website.

3. Students record the growth of the plants and communicate the changes in the plants each week, i.e., that they have flowers, germinated, made seeds, etc.

4. Students think of a research question to plan a plant experiment. For example: How much water does a plant need to grow well?

5. Students set up their experiments with the equipment provided, label, make repeats and record results in a table every week.

This eight-week unit introduces primary school students to the practices and skills that structure the scientific method: research, experiment, observation, measurement, recording, communication, inquiry, and questioning. This is authentic learning with real-life application, since the students take part in a 'messy' experiment that helps them to better understand the impact of soil type, water, and PH levels on plant growth. They are expected to create a video journal to communicate their findings about plant growth.

Extension Activity: Adopt a Plant, Flower, Tree, Animal. Apart from the scientific temper, the hands-on experience of observing plant growth also introduces **the vital emotion of caring – for our plant world, for our environment, for our planet**. It coheres with what the Dutch educator, Gert Biesta, calls the "existential dimension" of teaching, where students confront the world and our relation to it. **Adopting a plant, flower, tree or animal extends this connection well beyond the school years**. Schools could also consider gardening and farming as an element in "experiential education", taking a cue from the growing practice of urban farming in some cities.

Observing and caring for another member of the planet builds the recognition that each grows at its own pace and begins to move us away from an "egological" attitude (Biesta). We begin to understand and respect another, slower tempo, an antidote to our accent on speed and rapid solutions. **We can build the basis for a truly world- or planet-centred education** (Biesta). The dialogue between scientific knowledge and ethical imperatives sows the seeds for responsible action in teenage years and beyond.

The Magic of Moss and the Art of Attentiveness to Life at all Scales: Robin Wall Kimmerer

Brain Pickings (weekly newsletter by Maria Popova), June 18, 2020.

"In *Gathering Moss: A Natural and Cultural History of Mosses* — an extraordinary celebration of smallness and the grandeur of life, as humble yet surprisingly magical as its subject — botanist Robin Wall Kimmerer extends an uncommon and infectious invitation to drink in the vibrancy of life at all scales and attend to our world with befitting vibrancy of feeling.

One of the world's foremost bryologists, Kimmerer is a scientist blessed with the rare privilege of belonging to a long lineage of storytellers — her family comes from the Native American Bear Clan of the Potawatomi. **There is a special commonality between her heritage and her scientific training — a profound respect for all life forms, whatever their size** — coupled with a special talent for rendering that respect contagious.

Mosses, to be sure, are scientifically impressive beyond measure — the amphibians of vegetation, they were among the first plants to emerge from the ocean and conquer the land; they number some 22,000 species, whose tremendous range of size parallels the height disparity between a blueberry bush and a redwood; they inhabit nearly every ecosystem on earth and grow in places as diverse as the branch of an oak and the back of a beetle. But beyond their scientific notoriety, mosses possess a kind of lyrical splendour that Kimmerer unravels with enchanting elegance — splendour that has to do with what these tiny organisms teach us about the art of seeing.

'We poor myopic humans, with neither the raptor's gift of long-distance acuity, nor the talents of a housefly for panoramic vision. However, with our big brains, we are at least aware of the limits of our vision. With sophisticated technology, we strive to see what is beyond us, but are often blind to the myriad sparkling facets that lie so close at hand. We think we're seeing when we've only scratched the surface. Attentiveness alone can rival the most powerful magnifying lens.

Mosses and other small beings issue an invitation to dwell for a time right at the limits of ordinary perception. All it requires of us is attentiveness. **Look in a certain way and a whole new world can be revealed**.

Learning to see mosses is more like listening than looking. A cursory glance will not do it. Starting to hear a faraway voice or catch a nuance in the quiet subtext of a conversation requires attentiveness, a filtering of all the noise, to catch the music. Mosses are not elevator music; **they are the intertwined threads of a Beethoven quartet.** Knowing the mosses enriches our knowing of the world'.

The remarkable diversity of moss varieties known and named only adds to the potentiality for intimacy with the world at all scales. But among this vast multiplicity of mosses is one particular species inhabiting the small caves carved by glaciers into the lakeshore, which alone embodies immense wisdom about the mystery and meaning of life. Kimmerer writes:

'*Schistostega pennata*, the Goblins' Gold, is unlike any other moss. It is a paragon of minimalism, simple in means, rich in ends. So simple you might not recognize it as a moss at all. The more typical mosses on the bank outside spread themselves to meet the sun. Such robust leaves and shoots, though tiny, require a substantial amount of solar energy to build and maintain. They are costly in solar currency. Some mosses need full sun to survive, others favour the diffuse light of clouds, while *Schistostega* lives on the clouds' silver lining alone'.

This singular species subsists solely on the light reflections emanating from the lake's surface, which provide one-tenth of one percent of the solar energy that direct sunlight does. And yet in this unlikely habitat, *Schistostega* has emerged as a most miraculous jewel of life:

Source: nawwal.org (accessed 9.6.2021).

As Kimmerer observes, this tiny moss is a master of "the patient gleaming of light" — and what is the greatest feat of the human spirit, the measure of a life well lived, if not a "patient gleaming of light"? The humble, generous *Schistostega* illuminates the darkness of mere being into blazing awe at the miracle of life itself — a reminder that our existence on this unremarkable rock orbiting an unremarkable star is a glorious cosmic accident.

To pay attention, indeed, is the ultimate celebration of this accidental miracle of life. Kimmerer captures this with exuberant elegance:

'The combination of circumstances which allows it to exist at all are so implausible that the *Schistostega* is rendered much more precious than gold. Goblins' or otherwise. Not only does its presence depend on the coincidence of the cave's angle to the sun, but if the hills on the western shore were any higher the sun would set before reaching the cave... Its life and ours exist only because of a **myriad of synchronicities** that bring us to this particular place at this particular moment. **In return for such a gift, the only sane response is to glitter in reply".**

Photographs: Moss, Tree Roots, and Tranquillity at Angkor, Cambodia. Credit: author

My visit to the magnificent monuments at Angkor in Cambodia revealed the dramatic relationship between nature and humans, Braudel's geographical and civilizational cycles of time. The Khmer created a civilization of remarkable grandeur and aesthetic splendour from the 9th to 13th centuries C.E. , a synthesis of Hindu and Buddhist practices. After their decline, the dense tropical forests began to reclaim their domain, and it required the dedicated passion of French naturalists, writers, and conservators as well as Cambodian worshippers in the 19th century to restore the glories of Angkor for the benefit of humanity. However, the forces of nature continue to make their presence felt here, enhancing the aura and magic of the place.

Moss adds a sheen to serene faces in meditation. Perhaps they contemplated on the fragility and transience of life, yet the possibilities of a pleasing concord with the forces that shape our existence. A monk finds pensive tranquillity amidst the lush greenery at Angkor today. Certainly, trees and human ingenuity continue in a symbiotic dance, for removing the roots would ensure a collapse of the surviving masterpieces. This partnership is a lesson in humility, the limits of human striving, as much as a creative delight for the photographer's lens!

Immersions in Nature:

Claude Monet (1840-1926), Water Lilies

From the Musee de l'Orangerie in Paris:
https://www.youtube.com/watch?v=6fHorNn2zqQ
July 21, 2011. Accessed: 10.10.2020

From the Museum of Modern Art in New York:
https://www.youtube.com/watch?v=zEUylRqJXNY
September 30, 2020. Accessed: 10.10.2020

Monet, the French Impressionist master, captures simultaneously the ephemeral and transient in nature as much as its monumental presence. His art "offered a new kind of experience to the viewer, an extended encounter with a sequence of successive perceptions that seemed to go beyond the limits of conventional painting. Never before had the spectator had such access to the nuances of an artist's sensibility, nor had the possibility that the passage of time might itself become the object of painting been so dramatically made evident" (Kendall 18).

Painted during his later years, and using the large gardens in front of his house at Giverny as a source of motifs, the series of canvases entitled "*Water Lilies, Water Landscapes*" became some of his most ambitious and extensive works, according the viewer a uniquely immersive experience: "the artist had taken up a vantage point above the surface of the water, painting little but the flowers and leaves and their watery environment. Progressively the artist sets us adrift in the indeterminate spaces of the pond, surrounded only by lily-pads and reflections of the sky...we find ourselves cut off from the conventional experiences of art, from the certainties of perspective and the comforts of familiar subject matter" (Kendall 20).

With Monet, we are absorbed into the narrative of nature, its subtle shifts of tint and mood, each detail taking on a character of its own. We are also plunged into the mysteries and wonders of creation itself, both of the artist and of the elemental forces that he depicts.

Learning Activity: Painting Water Lilies

For first time painters or school students:
https://www.youtube.com/watch?v=hnR5sXKCU0U
January 28,2020. Accessed: 11.10.2020

For adults or more experienced painters, there are options in oil and acrylic:
https://www.youtube.com/watch?v=YpmdlAi0IUY
May 14, 2013. Accessed: 11.10.2020
(David Dunlop in Givenchy; oil painting)

https://www.youtube.com/watch?v=W13RvLaJUuI
September 10, 2019. Accessed: 11.10.2020
(Jon Sephton at Galerie JS, Monflanquin, France; acrylic).

William Wordsworth – Nature Heals and Changes Perspective

On his travel through the English Lake District in September 2000, the philosopher and founder of the "School of Life", Alain de Botton, recalled the impact of Nature on the poetry and life of William Wordsworth (1770-1850), a former denizen of that delightful corner of the world. The elation that Wordsworth expressed in his intimacy with the natural world was not, in de Botton's words, "haphazard articulations of pleasure", rather "a well-developed **philosophy of nature**…the poet proposed that Nature, which he took to comprise…birds, streams, daffodils, and sheep, was an indispensable corrective to the psychological damage inflicted by life in the city" (de Botton 136). In an insight with deep resonance to our times, more urbanized and frenetic than his, "the poet accused cities of fostering a family of life-destroying emotions: anxiety about our position in the social hierarchy, envy at the success of others, pride and a desire to shine in the eyes of strangers"; during his residence in London, Wordsworth was as baffled as we are of "how lived even next-door neighbours, yet still strangers, not knowing each other's names" (138-39). The pandemic of loneliness had set in with the arrival of industrial society.

Remarkably similar to the Chinese *Dao de Jing*, which fused the "way" of Nature with human virtue, Wordsworth expressed his appreciation for its shaping of a "higher self" in *The Prelude*:

If, mingling with the world, I am content
With my own modest pleasures, and have lived
                                                   …removed

From little enmities and low desires,
The gift is yours…
Ye winds and sounding cataracts! 'tis yours,
Ye mountains! Thine, O Nature!

The contrast of city and countryside leads de Botton to suggest that "we accept a prior principle: that our identities are to a greater or lesser extent malleable; that we change according to whom – and sometimes *what* – we are with" (147). This also calls for a shift in viewpoint; moving between the human and natural perspective could be inspiring "perhaps because unhappiness can stem from having only one perspective to play with" (150). In Braudel's parlance, connecting with different cycles of time contributes to an amplifying of human possibility and a "fluid intelligence" which includes **the notion of "multiple identities"**. We can move beyond cultural conditioning and constraints, becoming comfortable with and celebrating an expanded self.

In my personal experience, the link with nature is the source of endless joy. Growing up amidst the tea plantations of Assam in Eastern India, surrounded by jungle and a cornucopia of plants and animals, gifted me a childhood of immense wonder and rapture. Even as a confirmed urbanite today, that sense of connectedness continues in resounding chords. On a recent visit to the Scottish highlands, I could feel the surge of delight that Wordsworth had so poetically penned more than two centuries ago.

Photos: Scottish highlands. Credit: author.

I was reminded here of the observation from Zen:

The mountain flows
The river sits

Nature always opens the door to shifting perspectives, to a transcendent understanding.

Contemplation of Nature: the Dry Zen Garden
Ryoanji Temple, Kyoto, Japan

Google Images: Ryoanji Zen Temple

Traditional gardens in Zen temples in Japan are usually dry, composed of large rocks surrounded by carefully raked gravel in flowing forms. These elements have symbolic significance, with rocks representing solidity or "the true nature of things as they appear " and the gravel signifying "the impermanence of flowing water" (Simpkins 69). They could also be viewed as complementary aspects of movement and rest, a mirror image of the mind itself.

Learning Activity: Create a Dry Zen Garden (for all ages)

The space required is minimal, a small section of the field or yard in a school or at home. Older and worn rocks are preferred as containers of "chi" or energy. The gravel should be light in colour and texture, and should be spread over the surface before placing the rocks. The placing of the objects is an individual or group decision, without any preconceived notions.

After completing the garden, invite your classmates or neighbours to comment on the interplay of elements and to look at multiple perspectives that may emerge. Or simply contemplate the garden in silence.

Movement is our first language: 3-year old Jonathan sways to Beethoven's Fifth Symphony

https://www.youtube.com/watch?v=0REJ-lCGiKU
March 15, 2010. Accessed: 5.11.2020

The three year old "conducts" part of the final movement of Beethoven's Fifth Symphony, which is a triumphant statement of overcoming adversity. The well-known four note opening of the symphony has been interpreted as a "knocking of Fate", perhaps an expression of Beethoven's anguish at the onset of deafness that would haunt the rest of his life. In the "Heiligenstadt Testament", he wrote of his struggle with the impairment and contemplating suicide; luckily for humanity, he willed himself forward and gifted us some of the greatest expressions of the soul. The Fifth Symphony tracks this journey from challenge to an exultation of the human spirit.

Jonathan gives us his joyful 'rendition' here, moving in remarkable concordance with the notes and rhythm; he is "conducting" the energy and creative spark through his being, he has become the music. As T.S. Eliot expressed it in "The Dry Salvages":

music heard so deeply
That it is not heard at all, but you are the music
While the music lasts.

Movement is indeed our first language, uniting us across cultures and ages. It is also the essential accompaniment to a sense of lifelong wellbeing.

Learning Activity: Move with Beethoven, Move with Rap

Many schools begin the day with some form of physical movement, an energizing tonic for the body and mind. This practice should become part of our daily repertoire. Whether one moves to the changing rhythms of a Beethoven symphony or to the zestful beats of Rap, music and movement become the conduits for a rush of endorphins, our feel-good and euphoric chemicals.

Learning Activity: Moving with Morning Bright Light

Stanford University neuroscientist Dr. Andrew Huberman emphasizes the importance of regulating our body-brain connection through physical movement and controlled respiration. Among the biggest changes in health behaviour he recommends is getting **two to ten minutes of bright light on waking**, which helps to organize our nervous system and has positive effects on physical, mental, digestive, and immune aspects of health (Huberman). The Indian Yoga tradition of mind-body wellness incorporated this insight in a series of movements and breathing patterns called the "Surya Namaskar" or "Sun Salutation", now validated by neuroscience.

"Surya Namaskar", The Sun Salutation
Rashmi Ramesh explains the twelve steps of the exercise:
https://www.youtube.com/watch?v=AbPufvvYiSw
June 8, 2016. Accessed 7.11.2020

A Paean to Nature: Beethoven Symphony no. 6, "Pastoral"
Columbia Symphony Orchestra. Conductor: Bruno Walter.

www.youtube.com/watch?v=LFFSdNVZ58E&t=130s
July 17, 2017(recorded January 1958). Accessed: 7.11.2020

In this magnificent symphony, Beethoven expresses our captivation with the delightful vistas of nature, its transient moods and power, and our sense of connectedness to its rhythms. In the first movement, which he called "awakening of cheerful feelings upon arrival in the countryside", we feel the gush of delight at entering a landscape of trees, flowers, and birds. There are many repetitive sounds, but repetition in nature amplifies joy and harmony! Beethoven transports us to a tranquil and flowing "scene by the brook" in the second movement, ending with the trills of cuckoos and nightingales. We are then treated to "a merry gathering of country folk" in the third movement, a celebration of rustic pleasures, which is dramatically disrupted by the howling winds, crashing thunder, and the gushing downpour of a storm. Calm and serenity are restored in the final moment as a shepherd's song intones "cheerful and thankful feelings after the storm". Beethoven's exquisite voicing of the dynamic cycle of nature is encased in gratitude at its abundance, a source of eternal nourishment.

SOURCES/CITATIONS

Biesta, Gert. "The Beautiful Risk of Education".
https://www.youtube.com/watch?v=QMqFcVoXnTI&t=2647s
June 8, 2017. Accessed: 15.7.2020

de Botton, Alain. 2002. *The Art of Travel.* London, Penguin.

Gelb, Michael J. 1998. *Think Like Da Vinci.* London, Harper Element.

Hossack, Rebecca. "The Wonders of Australian Aboriginal Art". TedX Oxford.
https://www.youtube.com/watch?v=2vYv3nfMmFU
May 29, 2020. Accessed: 27.9.2020

Huberman, Andrew. "Growth Mindset Biohacks".
https://www.youtube.com/watch?v=OGa_jt3IncY
May 21,2020. Accessed: 18.8.2020

Jones, Colin. "What do Circles Represent in Aboriginal Art?"
https://www.youtube.com/watch?v=qyUxxgwHK8Q
October 18, 2013. Accessed: 29.9.2020

Kendall, Richard, ed. 2004. *Monet By Himself.* London, Time Warner Books.

Lu, Yanying. "Water Metaphors in *Dao de Jing*: A Conceptual Analysis". Open Journal of Modern Linguistics. 2012. Vol.2, no.4, 151-158.

Simpkins, Annellen and C. Alexander Simpkins. 2003. *Zen in Ten.* Boston, Tuttle.

The Second Circle of Joy

The uncoiled energy from the first circle flows into forces of procreation and fertility at the second, centred at the lower abdomen. As the origin of life, breath can be cultivated to circulate harmoniously in the body, moving from intense animation to deep rest. We rely upon well rooted practices in some of our oldest civilizations to enhance foundational potency and wellbeing. We can also draw inspiration from their unbounded delight in the union of sensual and erotic vitality, manifested in an aesthetic outpouring that continues to enchant a millennium later. The profusion of natural and human creation finds its echo in the greater tolerance of variation in sexual and gender identities in our times. However, the joy of acceptance remains tempered by the obstacles faced in many parts of the world against the freedom of personal choice.

Aware as well of the limitations of our senses in comparison to other species, we nevertheless exult in the incredible thrill of engaging the world with them. Sensory perception is the foundation for our remarkable achievements in scientific study and artistic imagining. Fuelled by our insatiable curiosity, this exploration shares the playfulness of childhood inquiry. We examine how aspects of play and gamification in school and the workplace may restore the feelings of wonder and spontaneity in all spheres.

This circle heightens the joy of movement, our first and natural language, in the exuberant steps of dance. From the very beginning, humans have expressed every range of emotion in dance, a coalition of body, mind, and spirit. Often associated with revelry and festivity, it may sometimes also become a balm in the most challenging circumstances, playing a vital role in healing as people recover from the traumas of war, injury, or illness. It may also become our faithful ally in healthy aging. **This is a joy born from resilience and renewal.**

The leitmotif of **connectedness** continues in this circle, encompassing the self and others. Tapping into the enormous energy resources within our own body sets us on the journey to exploration and admiration of civilizational achievements from different corners of the world, while nature remains a constant source of inspiration. On a practical level, we look at the complexities of relationships in an era of rapid change tempered with social conventions from the past, and the necessity of educating students and adults in this key domain of well-being.

The learning activities extend an examination of our "mental maps" with a spatial dimension. Curiosity, observation and creativity are combined with playful forays in art and into the imagination in encouraging the emergence of young authors and storytellers. **We also introduce the vital element of reflection, the catalyst for a lifelong mindset of contemplation and growth.**

Listening remains a central skill, and when integrated with movement, becomes a powerful stimulus to relational learning. We complete the circle on an appropriate note of zestful union.

Centring Energy: "*Dan Tian*" breathing

In remarkable anticipation of the current scientific understanding of the origin of life in the "Big Bang", Chinese Daoists affirmed the transformation of "*Wu Chi*" or the vast void into "*Tai Chi*" or the infinite energy of the Universe (Lam). The infinity divided into the "*Yin*" for storing energy and the "*Yang*" for expressing energy, but these are clearly complementary forces and much of Chinese philosophy and practice hallowed "*Yinyang*" to capture the cosmic and human drama of unity and separation. Daoism played a seminal role in traditional Chinese medicine and healing, based on the insight that the unity of external and internal energy fields could pave the way to an extended and healthy human lifespan. In other words, we could live longer and better, which resonates agreeably in our era of expanded life expectancies.

In common with other curative and wellness traditions, such as Indian *Ayurveda* and *Yoga*, the Chinese begin with the vitality of our foundational lifeforce, the breath. To flow and flourish within the human body, the breath must partake of the boundless vigour of universal energy with a "commander" or coordinator located at the central point of our anatomy. That is the lower *"Dan Tian"* (*Tanden* in Japanese), which translates in Chinese as the "elixir of the rice field", a poetic metaphor for the essence of fertility and vitality[4] (Lam). An invisible spot about three finger lengths below the belly button and a similar breadth inside, located between the waist and the perineum, the *"Dan Tian"* is indeed the incubator of our procreative and sensual energy. To centre the breath in this area is to tap into the vast resources of universal *"Qi"* (or *"Chi"*), a source of circulating pleasure and wellbeing in the body and the mind.

Learning Activity: *"Dan Tian"* Breathing (for all ages)
www.youtube.com/watch?v=4WJbpL_kwNs&t=301s
May 18, 2019. Accessed: 12.11.2020

"Dan Tian" Breathing Meditation (for older students and adults)
https://www.youtube.com/watch?v=hpBqddaYT7s
February 13, 2017. Accessed: 17.7.2020

"Dan Tian" breathing is a vital ingredient in an entire system of health maintenance in Chinese culture called *"Qigong"*. It includes a series of

---

4   In English, it is often translated as the "lower heaven", which captures the sense of enormous wellbeing that accompanies the harmonious circulation of energy within the body.

movements that enhance the flow of energy in the body, based on observation and understanding of "meridians" that affect different parts of
the anatomy. Unlike the martial arts, which require intense discipline
and rigorous practice, *Qigong* routines are relatively easy to practice and
master. My personal experience with *Qigong* has been extremely beneficial in creating a state of calm and quiet exaltation as the body achieves
a centring and a surge of harmonious vigour. Although there are endless
options, I prefer a routine which includes chest opening and deep lung
exhalation exercises, apposite in the Covid era and beyond.

**Learning Activity: *Qigong* Routine – "*Immuni Qi*" for Lungs and
Immune System (for all ages)**
https://www.youtube.com/watch?v=BC9MvsxZrW4
March 19, 2020. Accessed daily since 15.6.2020

In this video (40 minutes) *Qigong* practitioner Jeff Chand leads us
through a series of movements, including "*dan tian*" breathing, energy
circulation, tapping and massage of meridian points for the immune
system like the "*hegu*" and the "*baxie*" in the hands and the "*fengchi*"
at the base of the skull (considered the entry point for pathogens). The
body and the mind are trained for resilience. There is also an invitation
to join the online community of "*Communi Qi*" as a forum for further
learning on *Qigong*.

Resting Energy: "*Yoga Nidra*"

While the amplification of energy may be considered the "*Yang*" of daily
practice, it must be complemented with the "*Yin*" of relaxation and rest.
In the fast paced, restless rhythms of contemporary living, heightened
levels of anxiety and stress contribute to insomnia and other painful
states of acute discomfort. In a remarkable synthesis of modern science
and ancient practice, the Stanford University neuroscientist Dr. Andrew
Huberman recommends "*Yoga Nidra*" as a path towards the re-wiring

of the brain into a state of deep rest (Huberman). An Indian method dating back more than a thousand years, the technique guides us into the *Theta* and *Delta* brainwave states, which represent a slowing and regeneration of the brain. It may be particularly helpful in advancing years, for *Theta* and *Delta* activity are known to decrease as we age, resulting in sleep problems that *Yoga Nidra* could help in tackling. Yoga therapist Richard Miller developed the "Integrative Restoration" (iRest) methodology based on *Yoga Nidra* in a variety of settings including military bases, veterans' clinics, homeless shelters, Montessori schools, Head Start programmes, hospitals, hospices, chemical dependency centres, and jails; the protocol was also used with American soldiers returning from the Afghanistan and Iraq wars and suffering from post-traumatic stress disorder or PTSD (Wikipedia). **High school and university students may find it particularly beneficial in their competitive, high stress environments.** It is a reminder that endorphins, our "feel good" chemicals, are also in essence "pain killers"!

Learning Activity: *Yoga Nidra* **(for older students and adults): 30 minutes**
https://www.youtube.com/watch?v=SNF88XoqnP0
April 23,2020. Accessed: 13.11.2020

Explosive Energy: Erotic Sensuality and Artistic Exuberance at Khajuraho, India

The intense forces of fertility and procreation have been worshipped and celebrated from the beginnings of human existence, none more so than in our earliest cultures and in the creative outpouring of Indian civilization. The stunning sculptural walls of the Khajuraho temples in Central India, built in the 9th and 10th centuries C.E., offer an uninhibited panorama of human vitality in a state of utter plenitude and pleasure. Sex and eroticism, far from being negated or regarded with moral disdain, were seen as joyful instincts and sources of unbounded delight. They represent a synthesis of two essential strands of Indian thought and practice: the unrepressed sexual customs and fertility cults of indigenous peoples with the Hindu understanding of the human drama as a microcosm of the cosmic theatre. In a remarkable echo of Chinese Daoism, Creation was viewed as the union of complementary forces, in this case female and male, reproduced (quite literally!) in human procreation, both acts endowed with elements of rapture and bliss. Importantly, for the Hindus, the active emanation of energization arose from "*Shakti*" or the feminine force. The walls at Khajuraho are replete with the beauty and fecund power of women, whether as the goddess, or the intimate human companion, but almost always in partnership with the male, a "striving for completeness and fullness of life" (Smith 186). They also honour the Hindu conception of Creation as a "*lila*" or playful sport of the Gods, introducing "elements of spontaneity and freedom into the universe" (207). The variety of erotic practices depicted here partakes of this spontaneous license, but without a trace of vulgarity, for the faces are bathed in a serene joy.

Divine creation and biological procreation find their natural counterpart and culmination in human creativity. Music and dance spring from every corner in Khajuraho and we are swept along in the tide of euphoria from each note and step. These artists understood that eroticism endows the human imagination with infinite vibrancy, and our passion for the arts imbibes from the same exalted well.

Khajuraho photographs. Credit: author

Erotic and Relational Intelligence:
Esther Perel, psychologist and relationship therapist:
"Erotic Intelligence: the paradox of intimacy and sexuality"
https://www.youtube.com/watch?v=Iepv0NpdSOM
July 27, 2012. Accessed: 14.11.2020

Khajuraho presents us with an idealized picture of union and fulfilment, both sexual and emotional. The reality of human relationships is far more complex, requiring skilful navigation. Psychologist, Esther Perel, presents a poignant tale of her parents as concentration camp survivors; brought up in Antwerp, Belgium; she contrasts those survivors "who did not die and those who came back to life". Her family is a sterling example of the latter; based now in New York, she helps others to steer through the challenges of contemporary partnerships, covering a spectrum that reflects the "sexual fluidity" and identities of our times. She explains the relatively recent historical shift from notions of community belonging and status, to the "Western" emphasis on the individual, where the partner is seen as "best friend, trusted confidante, and passionate lover" (a trend which is now visible in many urban, non-Western settings as well). Not surprisingly, this could lead to overlapping or conflicting priorities in our relationships.

Perel highlights the tensions between the need for safety, intimacy, and connection on the one hand and the desire for passion, adventure and autonomy on the other. In an existential *"Yinyang"*, we must reconcile love and desire, the erotic and the domestic, sexuality and intimacy. In an echo of the spirited celebration of play in Khajuraho, she calls for a "paradigm switch", a re-discovery of the young child's sense of freedom and playfulness. Allied to this freedom is a feeling of separateness, and Perel sees this "space" or "gap" as essential to maintaining the spark in a relationship. Social scientists refer to the "porcupine effect" in human relationships – a large distance creates the chill of death, while extreme proximity leads to a piercing by the quills. Discovering "a comfortable distance" maintains some mystery and edge, necessary to the "erotic elan". Perel approvingly notes the French author, Marcel Proust's observation that "true discovery is not to go to new places, but to look with new eyes".

None of this can mask the reality that human relationships are often fraught and messy, with the sometimes alarming outcomes of separation, loneliness, and suicide ideation. **In my opinion, high school and university students should undertake mandatory guided conversations and lessons in "relational intelligence", a peculiar omission in most curricula today.**

Learning Activity: Listening (young adults and older)

Esther Perel's podcast, *"Where Should We Begin?"*, which includes anonymous sessions with couples and relationship questions.

Gender Identities and Orientations: Variation and Acceptance

Among the remarkable changes in human behaviour and attitudes in the last 50 years has been the growing recognition of a wide spectrum of sexual preferences and fluidity in gender identities, crowned by the legal acceptance of same-sex marriage in several countries, particularly in Western Europe and North America[5]. Despite a chequered history, and continuing intolerance in some cultures, the awareness and even celebration of sexual variation can be found in several indigenous cultures as well as ancient civilizations such as Greece, India, and Persia. The *"Kamasutra"*, an Indian text from the 4th century C.E., explores "*kama*" or "desire" in its infinite diversity, noting that *kama* "finds its finality in itself" (Vanita 46). The 14th century Persian poet, Hafiz, gives us a

---

[5] South Africa and Taiwan are the beacons in legalizing same-sex marriage in their respective continents.

beautiful glimpse of the possibilities of tolerance in *"It happens all the time in heaven"*.

"It Happens All the Time in Heaven"

It happens all the time in heaven
And some day it will begin to happen again
On Earth
That men and women who are married
And men and men who are lovers
And women and women who give each other light
Often will get down on their knees and while so tenderly
holding their lover's hand
with tears in their eyes
will sincerely speak, saying
My dear, how can I be more loving to you?
How can I be more kind?

In the land of the *"Kamasutra"*, homosexuality came to be viewed as a perversion and a criminal act with the imprint of foreign invaders and rulers, reversed after a long legal battle in 2018. Art and narrative, though, kept the flame alive and continue to document the changing histories of individuals as they reach toward personal fulfilment.

Mitylene in Bombay – by Inez Vere Dullas (in Vanita 346).

No Lesbos this, our sea-girt isle,
and Sappho does not sing
her songs of love with silvern tongue
yet nonetheless they still are sung
by voices new, in tropic clime.

Removed from ancient Grecian time
in dim cafes they meet –
svelte versions of the classic gay,

they come to watch the cabaret
perchance to cruise the clientele.

And some fall victim to the spell
the Tenth Muse used to weave
that now is woven by the girls
in slacks, who smile through blue smoke whorls
their message, while the music plays.

Dubious – by Vikram Seth (in Vanita 326).

Some men like Jack
and some like Jill;
I'm glad I like
them both; but still

I wonder if
this freewheeling
really is an
enlightened thing –

or is its greater
scope a sign
of deviance from
some party line?

In the strict ranks
of Gay and Straight
what is my status?
Stray? Or Great?

LGBTQ+ Storytelling in the Digital Age
Nathan Manske, Google Talks
https://www.youtube.com/watch?v=tAgKM-9iEac
March 6, 2018. Accessed: 7.10.2020

Nathan Manske launched the *"I'm from Driftwood"* website in 2009, which documents LGBTQ stories from across the USA. Driftwood is the small town in Texas where he grew up, and he was inspired by the scene in the film *"Milk"* where Harvey Milk used the poster, "I'm from Woodmere, New York". Small towns and rural areas may be seen as particularly challenging for LGBTQ individuals because of their isolation and seeming conservatism on matters of gender orientation, so the website wanted to reassure them that "you're not alone". Although it began with the goal of storytelling about youth experiences, the responses began to reflect an age spectrum, including tales of "coming out" at 60. Manske emphasizes, though, that the focus continues to be on the "queer experience" and how it is meaningful for the individual.

Storytelling always contains the unique capacity to build empathy with others and their lived reality. Scientifically, this can be linked to the activation of "**mirror neurons**" in the brain that create connections to the stories of others and reinforce the power of sharing. After travelling and documenting through all fifty states of the US over four months, Manske noticed a trend which challenged the perception that small towns were particularly difficult for LGBTQ in terms of family support or "coming out" in school. Rather, **the stories confirmed the great diversity and uniqueness of experiences, which can be seen as a trait of the human saga in all spheres.** The broadening of the demographic created space for a "history and change" section, *"What was it Like?"*, where elders recount moving from decades where they could be arrested for dancing with a person of the same gender to being able to marry them!

The internet age makes stories of the LGBTQ journey easily accessible to people across the country and the entire world, **another form of global connection**. Manske feels that online storytelling will become more de-centralized with the advent of Facebook and Instagram, drawing parallels to the multiple social media channels used by the "MeToo" movement to highlight instances of patriarchal domination and abuse.

Narrative can continue to be a powerful ally of greater tolerance and freedom from personal oppression in all corners of the globe.

Sensual Vibrance: Harnessing the Energy of the Senses

In her delectable and engaging *"Natural History of the Senses"*, Diane Ackerman points out: "Most people think of the mind as being located in the head, but the latest findings in physiology suggest that *the mind* doesn't really dwell in the brain but travels the whole body on caravans of hormone and enzyme, busily making sense of the compound wonders we catalogue as touch, taste, smell, hearing, vision" (Ackerman xix). Buddhists go a step further in describing the mind as the synthesizer of our sensory experiences, a possible sixth sense. These thoughts cohere well with the metaphors of circulation and dynamism in energy movement adopted in this book. Cultivating the senses is among the most delightful aspects of learning at any age, apart from founding the cornerstone of human achievements in scientific inquiry and artistic exploration. We may revel equally in privileging one sense, or in combining them in a heady synaesthesia.

Touch and Sound: A pianist describes the rapport with his instrument
Frank Denyer, English composer and pianist

"There are so many aspects to it. First a musical instrument immediately reflects the general state of one's physical/mental wellbeing, more than usually seeps into consciousness. I know from the first seconds of sitting down at the piano whether this is the start of a fruitful creative day, or merely one of keeping my muscles in shape and my mind on music. I know this from how aware I am of my fingertips on the keys. At the beginning of good days I am immediately and intimately sensitive to their surface and even their temperature, brain and fingertips are linked and at first I might take pleasure in slowly depressing just one key to sound a single very soft tone. On such days, I might also start by playing a chord of three random notes, again softly, and find pleasure in being able to make all the notes to sound precisely together (not as easy as you may think) just for the sensuous pleasure of it. But on other days I can't really be so bothered, I can feel the keys, of course, but not so immediately and I have to rely more on habit and muscular memory to get me through.

In playing one is trying to find a pathway through time, it is formed by a conjunction of muscular memory and 'being in the present'. This is a situation where looking ahead, or mentally reviewing something good or bad that has just passed, are traps for the unwary. One needs to stay strictly in the present. At the same time, there is another inner person who acts as listener and judge attempting to compare and repeal past experiences. **These two act in totally autonomous spheres separate from each other.** The physicality of playing is central and it alone mediates intention, habit, and memory" (Denyer).

Learning Activity: Connecting with a Musical Instrument, Sounds of Nature (for all ages).

Learning or listening to a musical instrument is a universal human trait, an enduring and endearing accompaniment to our species from its origins. In this activity, written or oral, we can detail our observations with particular attention to the sensations of touch and sound in interacting with the instrument (which could be the human voice), and the impact it has on our "mental map". We can **extend the activity** to describe the sounds of nature in our environment and the feelings that arise. **It is good to establish and renew the significance of careful listening at every opportunity, with beneficial effects on multiple aspects of learning.**

The Dilemma of Touch: Maternal Comfort and the Woman who Tickled Too Much

The awareness of touch has entered extensively into our lexicon from the "feelings" that we ascribe to emotions, to being deeply "touched" by an experience. Its complexity arises from the variety of experiences associated with the sensation. The "first touch" of maternal comfort can set the infant on a journey of emotional security and warmth, expanded upon later in pleasurable companionship and union with significant others. Indonesian culture keeps the young in a *"gendong"* carriage at the mother's hip for the first three years, and the Balinese child must not touch the earth for the first six months, being endowed with divine qualities. Not surprisingly, I haven't come across another culture to compare with the mellow friendly demeanour of Indonesians!

However, touch may become a source of exclusion or discomfort. In India, an entire social group were outcast as "untouchables" for the supposed "pollution" of their occupations, a form of discrimination that persists despite attempts at social and political change. A strange case in a British court in 1963 resulted in divorce because of the wife's complaint that her husband persisted in his demands that she tickle different parts of his anatomy: "Mrs. Lines complained to the court that he *even* demanded this when they were watching television. That, one can imagine, was just beyond the pale" (Herring 4). The wife developed acute anxiety and the judge noticed her hands moving in "involuntary tickling movements" in court; since the husband had persisted with his demands, Mrs. Lines was granted a divorce on the grounds of "cruelty". This behaviour has not escaped the attention of scientists; a group at the University of California discovered in their research that "tickling is an 'involuntary defence mechanism' that has developed through evolution. It is used to alert the brain to the fact that vulnerable parts of the body are being attacked. They suggest it is useful to distinguish two kinds of tickling: Garaglesis and Knismesis. The former is 'laughter associated tickling' and is a reflex reaction caused by heavy stroking of the skin. The latter, however, is caused by feather light movement across the skin which sends messages to the somato-sensory cortexes of the brain" (Herring 8).

Whether pleasurable, risible, discomfiting or tortuous, touch clearly remains a "ticklish matter".

The Remembrance, Fertility and Allure of Smell

Unlike touch, smell lacks a vivid vocabulary, leading us to resort to indirect expressions and comparisons. However, it does carry a powerful bond to our memory centres, linking us with familiar and intimate moments of the past. The salty flavours of our skin carry an atavistic association with our marine, oceanic origins. More humbly and intensely, the wafts of coffee and croissant, *naan* bread and *masala* (spicy) tea, turkey and cranberry sauce, conjure instants of cherished emotional warmth and belonging. The fragrance of incense seems to set us on a stairway to heaven in many cultures.

Learning Activity: Smell and Memory- Reflection (all ages)

Record and recount experiences with the smells of foods, perfumes, ceremonies, sport, animals and nature. In each case, establish a **sense of connection to others** and the emotions linked to the experience.

In my case, the wafts of exquisite aromas from the dahlias, sweet peas and nasturtiums in my mother's garden became the stepping stones to a lifelong exhilaration in nature's presence. The smell of a flower "reminds us in vestigial ways of fertility, vigour, life-force, all the optimism, expectancy, and passionate bloom of youth" (Ackerman 13). No one has captured the vibrancy and erotic undertones of flowers better than the American artist Georgia O' Keefe (1897-1996). Every painting of hers seems to enter into the innermost juice of the flower, conveying its generous availability for our delight.

Georgia O'Keefe: Flowers
https://www.youtube.com/watch?v=QeB4-iBJLtg
January 28, 2009. Accessed: 16.11.2020

Learning Activity: O'Keefe's Poppy Flower (for young students)
https://www.youtube.com/watch?v=HIhlnqR45FM
January 6, 2016. Accessed: 18.11.2020

Red Poppies Step by Step Acrylic Painting (for older students and adults)
https://www.youtube.com/watch?v=OeKT8luyqZE
January 16, 2020. Accessed: 18.11.2020

The staggering volume of the world's perfume industry attests to the allure of fragrance, as much for concealment of natural body odour as an indispensable ally in courtship and extended romance. Most appropriately, one of the exclusive brands, "Joy", combines the scents of rose and jasmine. A heightened expertise in smell, though, could stimulate the criminal mind as well, chillingly portrayed in the novel and film, "*Perfume*" (Suskind).

Taste: From Local to Global

Like smell, taste can transport us instantly into the emotional caress of childhood, the feeding and nourishment of early life that leaves a deep dietary and cultural imprint. It also binds us to the history of our species, since "culture began when the raw got cooked…when fire and food combined, an almost irresistible focus was created for communal life" (Fernandez-Armesto 5, 13). Cooking can be considered one of the great historical innovations, setting the basis for shared mealtimes and the pleasures of convivial dining that persist in much of our world. Ritual and symbolism enhance the aura and taste of food. In Malay and Indonesian culture, thanksgiving and celebrations for beginnings are always attended with rice. The "*nasi tumpeng*" in Indonesia mirrors the conical shape of a mountain; the tip or "summit" is considered sacred and either offered to the gods or to the most honoured guest. The Indonesian word for taste, "*rasa*", carries connotations of "the essence" of life and behaviour, guiding each generation toward the desired qualities of "*halus*" refinement in courtesy, decorum, and mutual respect. Dietary restrictions also sport an ethical ambience, from the "*kosher*" and "*halal*" of Jewish and Islamic practices, to the prohibition of beef for Hindus and Jains. A rising tide of vegetarianism and veganism in our times may be allied to the emergence of an "environmental ethic" which begins to confront the human paradox that "we must kill other forms of life in order to live" (Ackerman 172).

The advent of the microwave and "fast food" outlets threatens to undermine the communal aspect of eating: "food on the fly feeds the values of hustle, nourishes the anomie of post-industrial society...the loneliness of the fast-food eater is uncivilizing" (Fernandez-Armesto 22). On a more positive note, the "globalization of taste" has rescued bland German cuisine with Turkish seasoning and peppered the dull British palate with the spicy vibrations of its new national dish, "*chicken tikka masala*". The even hotter sensations of Thai and Korean have begun their tangy inroads. Some local delicacies, though, are unlikely to find their way on to the "global foodie" table; the "*Fugu*" or puffer fish, which contains the lethal poison tetrodotoxin that must be removed by a skilful chef, will likely remain a Japanese fascination at a brush with death.

Learning Activity: Tastes and "Mental Maps" – Reflection (all ages)

Record your observations (in a format of your choice) on food choices that have shaped your experiences. Were they formed by your own culture or by multiple stimuli? Extend the idea to the Indonesian concept of "*rasa*" – how is "taste" (good or bad) defined in your culture, and has it changed due to contact with other people? Have you changed your eating preferences due to personal, environmental, or planetary concerns?

How might these practices and decisions impact your "mental map"? (referred to in the "first circle").

Sight and Vision: Insurpassable Plenitude

Sight appears to be our dominant sense since "seventy percent of the body's sense receptors cluster in the eyes, and it is mainly through seeing the world that we appraise and understand it" (Ackerman 230). Terms like "viewpoint" and "worldview" seem to confirm the primacy of sight in evaluating our experiences, as do the positive ring of "foresight" and "vision". Yet, in common with the other senses, **the true delight of sight resides in the infinite variation, the cornucopia of perceptions, that arise from those sensors.** Scientists have magnified the power of sight to uncover the secrets of nature, ranging from the cosmic spectacle to the micro-brew of cells and tiny organisms, aiding human progress in fields as diverse as space, medicine, communications, technology, and entertainment. Artists continually challenge and extend our encounter with the familiar and the exotic so that we literally "see with new eyes". None more so, perhaps, than the French painter, Paul Cezanne (1839-1906), who is considered to be the bridge from the "traditional" to the "modern" in Western art.

Maurice Merleau-Ponty writes that "if the painter is to express the world, the arrangement of his colours must carry with it...the imperious unity, the presence, the insurpassable plenitude which for us is the definition of the real...Cezanne wanted to portray the world, to change it completely into a spectacle, to make *visible* how the world *touches* us" (in Ackerman 267).

Paul Cezanne: *In the Park at Chateau Noir* (1900)

Looking at this entrancing yet mysterious spectacle[6], Francoise Barbe-Gall observes: "Rocks, some trees, that is all: next to nothing. And yet this painting creates an entire world out of these few objects. Would it not be simpler and quicker to draw things as they are and give each of them their actual shape? The situation would then be clearer. And the path would open up of its own accord. **But that is precisely the point. We do not see things exactly as they are...**Cezanne tries to work as if he knows nothing and has never seen anything previously... The brushstrokes accumulate, sometimes superimposed on one another,

---

6 Image source: *reproduction-gallery.com* (accessed: 9.11.2020)

constructing the image. Taken in isolation, they represent nothing… but they convey as closely as possible what the artist gleans from nature" (Barbe-Gall 182). The image is restricted and indefinite, but Cezanne remained true to his representation of nature and "reality", enriching our "palette of being" along the way.

Sight and Sound: The Splash and Cadence of Seasons

Naoko Tosa – *Sound of Ikebana, the Four Seasons* (2013)
https://www.youtube.com/watch?v=7kqUpkyctOw
January 30, 2014 (Spring). Accessed: 18.11.2020

Japanese artist Naoko Tosa merges the traditional Japanese art of "*ike-bana*" flower arrangement with a video artwork in which sound vibrations are added to pastels and oil paints by shooting with a high speed camera at 2000 frames per second. The result is a mesmerizing flow of colours and tones that capture the changing hues and timbres of the seasons: palm and cherry in spring, cool water and morning glory in summer, red leaves in autumn, snow and camellia in winter. There is an erotic intensity to the splashes, as she enables us to enter the veins and the inner chemistry of nature, the source of fecund fulfilment. Like O'Keefe and Cezanne, Tosa edges us closer to a "truth", imperfect yet deeply pleasing.

The jaunty energy of play and gamification: re-discovering childhood spontaneity and imagination

Prof. Nancy Carlsson-Paige, Professor Emerita at Lesley University in Boston and author of several books on early education, including "*Taking Back Childhood*", bemoans the diminishing of play in schools. Play, as we saw earlier, nourishes our spontaneity and freedom, setting children on the path to building ideas, gaining social and emotional bonding, and using the imagination, "a mechanism for healthy growth", as universal as walking and talking (Carlsson-Paige). The reduction in play can be traced to the ubiquitous presence of "screen culture" and the commercial cross-marketing of products and media themes. What Carlsson-Paige observes as a result is young children playing out uniform and repetitive scenarios based on characters and stories promoted in multiple media. Moreover, the emphasis on testing and "benchmarking" standards for specific skills pushes early education toward teacher-led instruction and passive learning groups, but "only the most superficial and mechanical aspects of learning can be reduced to numbers" (Carlsson-Paige). This form of "drill" also generates a sense of failure in young minds as they struggle with "right" and "wrong" answers and singular paths to problem-solving.

We must restore the primacy of play in education at all levels to nurture the joy and love of learning. We would open the pathways to creativity and active, original thinking. Similar to plants and animals, humans grow at different rates and timescales, and play initiates a process of unique exploration and invention, balanced by an ambience of sharing and collaboration. Educators benefit too, as they partake in the blossoming of the natural capacities that they encounter and foster.

Learning Activity: Cultivating Characters (for younger students, adaptable to all ages)

Young authors enjoy creating stories, which allows full play to their imagination. This activity is done in pairs, in which one person can choose the role of "writer" and the other as "commenter", although they are reversible. It could also be done as oral storytelling. **The only limitation is that the characters must be animals, plants, or natural landscapes such as mountains, rivers, forests, and seas.**

After completing the story, the pair can choose materials to depict elements that would convey the essence, or they could choose to perform the scenario in an act. The focus is on sharing ideas without evaluation or judgement. **In personalizing the forces of nature we attempt to establish an early and lasting empathy with other lifeforms.**

Gamification fuels "fluid intelligence"

Gamification in our times has extended the benefits of play in multiple directions. As Yu-kai Chou points out, the demographic for gamification is generic, appealing to all ages. His concept of "octalysis" outlines eight "core drives" of motivators for gaming (Chou), which would be relevant in educational and work settings. "Epic meaning and calling" inspires a connection with something bigger than oneself. *Pain Squad*, for example, has children with cancer uploading their pain journals and literally "hunting down" their pain with the assistance of a police squad. With "development and accomplishment", players gain a sense of improvement and mastery in short-term tasks with long-term benefits: *Nike Plus and Fitbit* engender a habit of fitness that could become a lifelong commitment. The "empowerment of creativity & feedback" spans the thrilling combinations and strategies in *Lego* to the remarkable achievement of gamers in uncovering the AIDS virus protein structure within 10 days in *Fold It*, which had eluded scientists for 15 years (Chou). "Social influence and relatedness" enabled a power company in Canada to change behaviour by setting up a comparison of utility bills between neighbours, enabling a saving of 250 million dollars a year. "Unpredictability and curiosity" remain robust motivators, as evidenced in the *"Speed Cam"* lottery in Sweden. While those driving over the speed limit were fined, those who remained within the limit were entered into a lottery with a possibility of winning off the fines imposed on the speeders! The result was an overall reduction in speed of 20%, another instance of changed behaviour (Chou).

Gaming exhibits its utility in varied arenas. 10-year old Griffin Sanders guided the car driven by his great grandmother after she had a heart attack to prevent an accident with oncoming vehicles; when questioned by the police, he attributed it to his playing of *"Mario Cart"* (Zichermann). In the scientific field, *Eterna* aided in discovering new structures of RNA, the bio-mechanical blueprint of species, while *Phylo* uncovered 350,000 potential mistakes in the understanding of DNA genetic material. IBM's *City 1* enabled city managers to play with changing variables in tackling urban issues like traffic flows and waste management. In England, the Department of Work and Pensions, a large bureaucracy not known for innovation, introduced *Idea Street*. Ideas for improvement became a "stock" with virtual currency, redeemed by the "company". In the first 90 days, 1500 new ideas were generated, resulting in savings of 90 million pounds (Zichermann).

Gamification is clearly consonant with our post-industrial, information era, the "Conceptual Age" (Pink 2). Creativity, innovation, and the entrepreneurial spirit enable a fusion of work and play; "new ideas on the fly" breed a **fluid intelligence** designed around three F's – feedback, friends, and fun (Zichermann). The "winner effect" builds upon intrinsic reinforcement, for the more you succeed, the more you want to succeed, generating a "dopamine loop" of the feel-good chemical. **Most importantly, from an educational perspective, gaming is rooted in the idea of easy failure, preparing the ground for perseverance and grit.** Coupled with the social layer of team work and collaboration, these are powerful ingredients for an active engagement with learning at all phases of life. As work and play coalesce, we realize that "the opposite of play is not work but depression" (Kumar).

The primal energy of dance: biological drive, social connection, and healing

In the first circle, we looked at movement, allied to music, as our "first language". Not surprisingly, stepping into dance seems like a natural drive, an "expression of our hormonal and genetic makeup" (Lovatt). Contemporary science confirms the wide ranging benefits of dance. It organizes and strengthens brain connections, playing into its "plastic" capacity, and stimulates the reward centres. The joy of social interaction in dancing with others promises to reverse brain aging and decrease the risk of dementia (Neurogal), besides initiating greater empathy in coordinating moves with a partner. "Dance science" has emerged as a multidisciplinary area of study, combining physiology, anatomy, neuroscience, somatics (looking at the body-mind connection), and the arts (Rathle). The creative process of choreography prepares the ground for **educating the whole person**, generating the skills of non-verbal communication, problem-solving, decision-making, collaboration, adaptability, responsibility, clarity, focus, precision, and time management (Scrementi).

From our earliest societies, dance began to accompany every phase of life and expressed every emotion, from exuberant celebration to deep mourning. It continues to be an ally of healing in our times. Natalia Duong recounts how shared movement and "kinaesthetic empathy" helped the victims of "Agent Orange" poisoning in Vietnam to express their anguish and their hopes for the future. Bound to wheelchairs, with long lasting physical and cognitive disabilities due to the devastating impact of the defoliant used in bombing during the Vietnam War in the 1960's, they were able to emerge with movement when invited to tell their stories. The activation of "mirror neurons" in a shared activity help to move from sympathy for others to empathy with their story and to action. They eventually performed in Hanoi with a "choreography of falling and getting up", where each "fall" was followed by a determined forward motion (Duong). To me, this tale seems to symbolize the incredible resilience and fortitude of the Vietnamese that I witnessed on my visits there.

Every dance form carries a healing potential. In a study at McGill University in Canada, 40 participants with Parkinson's disease benefited from a 12-week course in **tango**, that bewitching fusion of African and Latin American rhythms. The melding of music, movement, and human touch of the partner makes tango a "pinnacle of synchronizing" which engages most of the brain (Rathle). Improvements in balance, functional mobility, and cognitive abilities were reported for the participants. Tango could make one an "oxytocin addict" at any age!

Learning activity: Choreographic mapping (for younger and older students)

In an extension of the "mental map" activities introduced earlier, students are asked to create their **biography in space** (ideally the classroom floor). These could include a representation of "home", of major landmarks of their life, as well as a projection of future dreams. They are then asked to move within the space and invite a partner to move with them while explaining the personal journey. Each person may select a piece of music or dance to accompany the movement. In mirroring the movements of others, we begin to amplify each other's life experiences, overcoming any language or ability barriers. This activity enables a rippling out of our common humanity.

Listening activities: Move with Dance and Music
The Best of Tango – with Astor Piazzolla
https://www.youtube.com/watch?v=-2Yn-epiMm0
April 14, 2015. Accessed: 23.11.2020

Piazzolla (1921-1992), the Argentinian composer, created a fascinating fusion between tango and classical music. This selection includes spring and autumn from the "Four Seasons", an echo of a similar piece by Italian composer Vivaldi three centuries earlier. It is highly recommended that each piece be danced with a partner!

Nutcracker Ballet – Dance of the Snowflakes
https://www.youtube.com/watch?v=fLKhWl3tEkk
October 18, 2019. Accessed: 20.11.2020

The perennial favourite of young and adults alike, the ballet by Russian composer, Piotr Tchaikovsky (1840-1893), transports us into the wonder world of childhood dreams, play, and enchanting landscapes. The dance of the snowflakes captures the mesmerizing spell of winter, and

Tchaikovsky's use of the human voice adds a touch of mystical innocence that pierces the inner child in us all.

Le Sacre du printemps (The Rite of Spring)
https://www.youtube.com/watch?v=EkwqPJZe8ms
October 2, 2017. Accessed: 24.11.2020

Although controversial at its opening in 1913, the *Rite of Spring* by Russian composer, Igor Stravinsky (1882-1971), is considered one of the seminal works of 20th century music. Subtitled "Pictures of Pagan Russia in two parts", the ballet sways with the rhythmic passion and erotic overtones of rituals celebrating the onset of spring and a "dance of the earth" which harks back to the worship of our natural home by early humans. Although the "sacrificial dance" in the second part may be less palatable to our sensibilities, this work is part of a reawakening of our sense of connectedness with, and guardianship of, the soil, which has taken on a new urgency in the 21st century.

Balinese Gamelan: The Love God and Goddess
www.youtube.com/watch?v=hQFlbqnvUqU&t=1429s
February 23, 2016. Accessed: 25.11.2020

The orchestra in the Indonesian Hindu island of Bali, called the "gamelan", usually consists of xylophone-like instruments or *"gangsas"*, bronze cymbals or *"ceng ceng"*, inverted bronze pots or *"riong"* and *"tromping"*, a flute or *"suling"*, and a pair of drums or *"kendang"*. Each instrument plays at its own tempo, yet there is a miraculous unity and harmony in the music, replicating the cycles of nature which attain completion within the flourishing of variation in each lifeform. This performance, by the *Gamelan Semar Pegulingan*, represents a revival of a rare classical type, where the *"gangsas"* are replaced by *"gender"*, a xylophone-like instrument where "the musician, seated on the floor, strikes the bronze keys with a mallet in each hand... in order to stop the sounds of the notes so that they won't run together, the player must lower his knuckles to touch the key after each note is played" (Eiseman 339). The dexterity of playing is matched by a delicate and sweet sound that will sweep you along in its heady tones. Fittingly, this selection celebrates the Love God of Bali, *Semara*, who is always paired with the Love Goddess, *Ratih*. As we witnessed at the walls in Khajuraho, Hindus rejoice in the union of the sexes, in the divine as well as human realms.

SOURCES/CITATIONS

Ackerman, Diane. 1995. *A Natural History of the* Senses. New York, Vintage Books.

Barbe-Gall, Francoise. 2010. *How to Look at a Painting.* London, Frances Lincoln.

Carlsson-Paige, Nancy. *Defending Play.*
https://www.youtube.com/watch?v=3FwDdjIQPZ4
July 14, 2015. Accessed: 20.11.2020

Chou, Yu-kai. *"Gamification to improve our world"*. Ted X Lausanne.
https://www.youtube.com/watch?v=v5Qjuegtiyc
February 26, 2014. Accessed: 18.9.2020

Denyer, Frank. *Personal communication with the author.* October 28, 2020.

Duong, Natalia. *"Dance as Therapy"* (TedX Stanford).
https://www.youtube.com/watch?v=J9gAe9H5Rok&t=2s
June 21, 2013. Accessed: 5.10.2020

Eiseman, Fred B.,Jr. 1990. *Bali Sekala & Niskala*. Vol. I. Jakarta, Periplus.

Fernandez-Armesto, Felipe. 2001. *Food: A history.* London, Macmillan.

Herring, Jonathan. 2009. *The Woman Who Tickled Too Much And Other Incredible Stories From Inside Britain's Law Courts.* Marlow, Pearson.

Huberman, Andrew. *Change Your Brain: Neuroscientist Dr. Andrew Huberman.*
www.youtube.com/watch?v=SwQhKFMxmDY&t=6045s
July 20, 2020. Accessed: 13.8.2020

Kumar, Janaki. *"Gamification at Work".* TedX Graz.
https://www.youtube.com/watch?v=6wk4dkY-rV0
January 12, 2015. Accessed: 20.9.2020

Lovatt, Peter. *Psychologist and Dancer* (TedX Observer)
https://www.youtube.com/watch?v=ihCh5wzNjYY&t=4s
April 12, 2012. Accessed: 4.10.2020

Neurogal MD. "Dancing is good for the brain".
https://www.youtube.com/watch?v=jYQ8QtonSKQ
March 14, 2019. Accessed: 4.10.2020

Pink, Daniel H. 2005. *A Whole New Mind.* New York, Riverhead Books.

Rathle, Karine. *"When Dance and Science Meet "*(TedX LSE).
https://www.youtube.com/watch?v=ylq7PZVSOvE&t=1s
October 22, 2013. Accessed: 5.10.2020

Scrementi, Cara. *"I believe in the power of dance"* (TedX UC Irvine)
https://www.youtube.com/watch?v=tbk1_K0bRrY
July 7, 2015. Accessed: 5.10.2020

Smith, V.A. 2011. *Khajuraho Unveiled.* Sydney, Greenage Books.

Suskind, Patrick. 1987. *Perfume.* New York: Alfred A. Knopf.

Vanita, Ruth and Saleem Kidwai, eds. 2001. *Same-Sex Love in India*. Delhi, Macmillan.

Zichermann, Gabe. *"The Future of Creativity and Innovation is Gamification"*. TedX Vilnius.
https://www.youtube.com/watch?v=ZZvRw71Slew
February 25, 2014. Accessed: 20.9.2020

The Third Circle of Joy

Centred in the navel, the third circle surges with the explosive potential of energy that originated in our first breath. The umbilical cord retains its mysterious aura, fuelling a lifelong bond with the forces that accompany us throughout our journey. We may appropriately consider this our "second brain", channelling and directing a vast swathe of actions and thoughts. The **vagus nerve** in fact creates a deep attachment between the intestinal tract and our cranial stem, which we refer to as the "gut-brain axis". If well conducted, this axis enables the flowering of the potential into harmonic chords of physical and mental vitality.

Our familiar friend, **movement**, returns in this circle with an added urgency as we confront the lifestyle illnesses borne from the current widespread curse of inactivity. Control and expansion of breath, emanating from, or adjacent to, the navel, is the foundation of traditional forms of body-mind wellness such as Yoga and Tai' Chi. Circulation of energy is further enhanced with a series of physical movements, and today we have accepted the notion of "embodied fitness" as the essential component of healthy vigour. Walking was the preferred mode in my grandparents' generation, and I'm happy to inherit that legacy, now bolstered with scientific evidence of its multiple benefits. The extension of movement into a propensity to wander takes on an additional thrill for a passionate traveller like myself. Here again, we can thank our nomadic ancestors, and the Hindu god Indra who proclaimed that "there is no happiness for him who does not travel". It is also comforting that the term *"vagus"* derives from the Latin "to wander", firmly linking our biology to a joyful propensity!

The leitmotif of **connectedness** finds a further boost in this circle too, bolstered by the findings of contemporary neuroscience. The benefits to the brain of physical exertion and healthy nutrition are well documented, covering the lifespan from immediate gain to long term prevention of debilitating illnesses. The "gut-brain romance", as Dr. Uma Naidoo calls it, enables a remarkable union of "macro" and "micro" ecology. Good eating choices reduce our reliance on industrial farming and its environmental harm, while also being friendly to the internal ecology of our biome.

At a grander level of connection, Greek thinkers such as Plato conceived of a universal "kosmos" of order and beauty, which found its echo in the "kosmos" of each individual mind and soul. Like all great minds, Plato achieved a synthesis of rational and intuitive thought, linking the complexity of the brain with the insight of the "gut instinct". The innate capacity of this instinct continues to power some of our most important and creative decisions, while also imparting the unrestrained pleasure of laughter.

The third circle heightens the joy of multiplicity and plurality, which will find ever greater impetus as we move up the energy cycle. Once again, we find a pleasing fusion of the "micro" and the "macro": our gut biome thrives on microbial diversity, and our greatest civilizations throughout the ages have flourished in diversity of thoughts, beliefs, and practices. **The "navels" of civilization highlighted here were predicated on the strength and beauty generated by the unlimited capacity for human ingenuity, exchange, and tolerance for difference.** They are powerful models for our globalizing era. As we search for the birthing of a new civilization, the Slow Movement urges us to rediscover our abiding ties to ecology and community, what Braudel terms the "longue duree" of geographical and historical cycles.

At this circle, we revel in the delights of wandering, exertion, good food, perceptive insight, jollity, variety, and of time itself.

"Sitting is the new smoking"

"Those who think they don't have time for bodily exercise will sooner or later have to find time for illness".

Edward Stanley

All human civilizations have realized and promoted the intimate link between physical movement and wellbeing. The elaborate systems of Yoga in India and Tai' Chi in China emerged from an understanding of the union of body and mind. Greek philosopher Plato warned that "lack of activity destroys the good condition of every human being, while movement and methodical physical exercise save it and preserve it". These insights take on added urgency in our sedentary age, stalked by an epidemic of physical inactivity, increasing levels of obesity, lifestyle diseases, and medical systems which are "poorly set up to encourage wellness" (Metzl). Just as science established the explicit link between cigarette smoking and a host of ailments, it has now confirmed that inactivity poses a perilous risk for human health. Sports medicine specialist Dr. Jordan Metzl calls for a conceptual change with physical activity and exercise becoming the basis for regenerative medicine and lifelong wellness. Contemporary neuroscience concurs, establishing connections between movement and the flourishing of several dimensions of the brain, as much as the prevention of cognitive decline in rapidly aging populations.

Neuroscientist, Dr. Wendy Suzuki, of New York University, Dr. Alvaro Pascual-Leone at Harvard Medical School and Dr. Daniel Corcos at Northwestern University validate studies that indicate changes in brain anatomy, physiology, and function arising from exercise regimens. In particular, the most transformative effects are palpable in the prefrontal cortex, which is critical for executive functions such as focus, attention, decision-making, and planning; the hippocampus in the temporal cortex, essential for long-term memory; and the amygdala, the deeper part of the brain that regulates emotion. The immediate increase in neuro-modulators such as dopamine, serotonin, and noradrenalin may explain the "feel good" factor flowing from physical exertion, with a longer term mood and energy boost (Suzuki).

Regular aerobic activity is known to have both acute (immediate) and chronic (continuous) impact across the lifespan, a vital ingredient in preventive medicine. Consonant with "neural plasticity", improved blood flow to the brain through exercise also triggers the growth of new blood vessels and cells, as well as protecting brain cells from degeneration, aided by BDNF, or the Brain Derived Neurotrophic Factor (Corcos). **Exercise thus appears to be an effective prevention for degenerative diseases like Alzheimer's and dementia (Metzl).** The benefits of physical activity, in fact, extend to amelioration of **every** disease; as Metzl points out, the data on exercise is more compelling than for diet and nutrition. The incidence of colon cancer reduced by 40% in those who exercised; a study in Norway found improvements in sleep patterns, self-esteem and memory and a decrease in anxiety among the participants (Metzl).

The scientific evidence of our times clearly echoes the understanding of our ancestors on the "embodied mind", the flowing and dynamic interaction of movement and cognition. With its 80 billion neurons and 100 trillion connections, the brain represents a network of movement and change par excellence. Taking the cue, the fitness industry today has undergone a paradigm shift toward "embodied fitness", with an emphasis on functional movement, strength, flexibility and mobility rather than "body building" (Minnino). The options for people of all ages are numerous. Yoga and Tai' Chi have both cognitive and emotional benefits, such as intensified grey matter in the brain for learning and memory, increased compassion and a decrease in fear and anxiety in the amygdala, complemented by relaxation through stimulation of the vagus nerve (Minnino). **Walking and running are well tested movements to generate functional connectivity in the prefrontal cortex and growth of new neurons with BDNF; when linked to group activity, they also contribute**

to communal bonding and an escape from social isolation. Aerobics and spinning set up the ability for convergent and divergent thinking underlying creativity, strength training is associated with decreased lesions in the brain's white matter, and high intensity interval training enables improved blood flow and cerebral vascular function (Minnino). At the **recommended frequency of 30 minutes each for 5 days in the week (150 minutes weekly),** at moderate intensity (50-70% of maximum heart rate), exercises that build flexibility and strength empower the connection of our muscles from tip to toe in the "kinetic chain" (Metzl).

There is clearly something for each one of us, at any age, to get us off the couch and into movement! At stake in this lifestyle choice are the benefits to public health, as much as in the motivation of extending the youthful state for the individual. We can draw inspiration from the French sculptor, Auguste Rodin's splendid *"Thinker"*, a well built and athletically fit symbol of the "embodied mind".

Rodin: *Thinker (Le Penseur)*[7]

---

[7] Image source: *nga.gov* (accessed 2.12.2020)

Learning Activity: Move with the Body Coach (all ages)

In his book, *"Spark"*, Dr. John Ratey of Harvard Medical School makes a strong case for bringing back play and exercise as a "stimulant modality" for learning, at schools and adult education alike (Ratey). During the enforced Covid lockdowns, Body Coach Joe Wicks posted a series of videos to help keep us moving, hopefully the beacon for a habit that lasts well beyond the pandemic[8]. A wide selection of workouts with clear explanations includes two examples for different age groups:

Kids Workout: 5 minute move
https://www.youtube.com/watch?v=d3LPrhI0v-w&list=PLyCLoPd4Vx-BvPHOpzoEk5onAEbq40g2-k

Low Impact Workout for Seniors: 15 minutes
https://www.youtube.com/watch?v=PWic8ckZ1q0

Eating Right: Embrace the "Gut-Brain Romance"

Along with physical exertion, food and nutrition become the foundational wellsprings of joyful living, relying upon informed choices. Even in an area of relative uncertainty and rapidly changing knowledge, the scientific fields of genetic epidemiology, nutritional psychiatry and neuroscience offer us prudent guidelines on healthy eating and positive mental states. Our enhanced understanding of the **"gut-brain axis"** must be attributed to the discovery of an entire universe within our bodies, **the microbiome,** a community of microbes or microbiota consisting of viruses, bacteria, and fungi, 99% of them living in our lower intestines. This "chemical factory" of 100 trillion microbes even outnumber our

---

[8] I am grateful to Andrew Thompson, my former colleague at Keystone Academy Beijing, for this source.

human cells, which comprise just 43% of our body! It is certainly worth cultivating them as friends, since they influence our mood, energy levels, immune system, and mental health. Studies on identical twins have confirmed that our microbiome is shaped to a large extent by environmental rather than genetic factors (Spector), reinforcing the importance of personal decisions in maintaining physical and cognitive wellness.

The microbiome journey starts at birth, but as an "acquired organ", it begins to crystallize over the first two years (Rossi). Rob Knight, co-founder of the American Gut Project, points out that a decrease in infectious diseases such as measles, mumps, hepatitis A and tuberculosis has been counter-balanced by a surge in microbiome-linked disorders, exemplified by the increased incidence of diabetes and the public health disaster of the obesity epidemic in several countries. By 2020, most American states reported obesity rates at above 30%, with the lowest hovering between 20-24% (Knight). The major culprit appears to be the combination of "fast" and processed foods that have swept over the dietary landscape in industrial societies, both "developed" and "developing". Prof. Tim Spector of King's College London points to the results of a **ten-day "burger binge"** diet that culminated in the loss of 1,200 types of bacteria, 40% loss in biome diversity, and long-lasting effects for two years. With the microbiome sequencing now visible in scientific study, **a range of diseases have been associated with a less diverse microbial community,** leading Spector to recommend the metaphor of an English country garden, blooming with a diversity of plants and greenery, for good gut health (Spector). **Variety does indeed turn out to be the spice of a robust life!**

As with movement, feeding our bodies well becomes a long-term investment in nourishing our brains and prevention of cognitive impairment. Dr. Lisa Mosconi, a neuroscientist, professor of nuclear medicine, and director of the Women's Brain Initiative at Weill Cornell, aptly affirms that successful brain aging appears to be "more diet than destiny". Brain scans reveal that those who consume at least 4 grams of DHA, one of the main types of Omega-3 fats, reduce the risk of Alzheimer's by 70% compared to an intake of less than 2 grams daily (Mosconi). Brain-friendly foods include salmon, sea foods, fish eggs, almonds, hazelnuts, walnuts, olive oil, flax and chia seeds, avocado, blue and blackberries, broccoli, green leafy vegetables, coconut oil, eggs, and dark chocolate (Mosconi, Kwik). Comprising 80% water, **the brain also thrives with adequate hydration**; just 2% de-hydration could lead to fatigue, confusion, memory lapse, and reduced attention span (Mosconi). The Chinese practice of consuming warm water at least an hour before or after meals appears ideal for vasodilation and absorption of fluids. In addition, research from the American National Institute of Health supports **adoption of "intermittent fasting"**, with a gap of 12 to 14 hours between the night and morning meal, since caloric restriction is positive for the brain (Mosconi). Here again, traditional norms in Indian culture anticipated neuroscience with regular weekly fasting, and Islamic cultures observe an annual month of fasting from sunrise to sunset.

Not surprisingly, processed foods, with their combination of trans saturated fats and cholesterol and excess copper, iron, and zinc cause harmful effects in the brain, doubling the risk of dementia, apart from inflammation of the heart (Mosconi). Nutritional psychiatrist Dr. Uma Naidoo promotes food as an "armour" against mental health concerns such as anxiety, depression, ADHD (attention deficit), and PTSD (post-traumatic stress), heightened during crises like Covid-19. She emphasizes the importance of a "holistic model" of healthy whole foods, a combination of Omega-3, vitamins D and E, colourful fruits and vegetables, and natural foods such as spices (Naidoo). Turmeric and black pepper, staples in the Indian diet, are increasingly adopted as anti-inflammatory protectors. Although nutrition remains a complex web of individual and cultural preferences, **evidence points to the multiple benefits of the diet perfected over centuries in the sunny lands of the Mediterranean.**

Dr. Megan Rossi, the "Gut Health doctor" and dietitian at King's College London, references an Australian study where over 30% of a group of moderate to severely depressed subjects placed on a Mediterranean diet for 12 weeks were no longer significantly depressed, as opposed to 8% in a placebo group, though both continued with medication (Rossi). MRI brain scans graphically illustrate the contrast of those on a Mediterranean diet and others on a "Western" diet dominated by "fast", highly processed foods and sugar: the former revealed tight ventricles that are protective for the brain, as well as a prominent hippocampus close to the "white matter" associated with neurogenesis (growth of new brain cells), while the brains of those on a "Western" diet showed larger and more expanded ventricles, and indications of shrinking and atrophy, especially in memory centres, considered a higher risk for Alzheimer's disease (Mosconi). **The brain-friendly Mediterranean diet certainly relishes a cornucopia of the earth's riches.** A daily intake of fruits, vegetables, grains, extra virgin olive oil, nuts, and dairy combines with weekly consumption of legumes, lean red meat, poultry, fish, and eggs, providing 50 grams of dietary fibre per day. The recommended quantity is 30 grams, while the typical British diet affords only 19 grams daily (Rossi). Apart from fibre, we need more polyphenols and fermented foods (Spector), and the Mediterranean diet scores well in these aspects too. Olive oil and red wine (particularly the chemical resveratrol) contain polyphenols or anti-oxidants, as do coffee, green tea, and dark chocolate, which is certainly good news for epicureans everywhere (in moderation, of course!). A Mediterranean dessert with Greek yoghurt delivers a delicious dose of fermented food, which can be supplemented with *kefir* (fermented milk) and *kombucha* (fermented tea), keeping our gut microbes well satisfied.

Food is, of course, more than simply a matter of the quality and quantity consumed; the rhythms of dining add a delectable element. Here again, the Mediterranean lands flourish in elegant and leisurely meals, flavoured with that most imperative ingredient: the bonds of conversation and laughter forged in community eating. My most memorable moments in Greece, Italy and Spain flowed from observing the elaborate rituals of evening meal preparations, preceded by the bonhomie of liquor and loud chatter. These are experiences of indescribable contentment.

Learning Activity: Cook a Mediterranean Meal

https://www.youtube.com/watch?v=VjlUcp4p1xQ
September 27, 2017. Accessed: 19.1.2021

Dietician Bill Bradley presents the ingredients of the Mediterranean diet from the island of Crete in Greece. This links us to the dawn of Greek civilization, since the Minoan culture of Crete could be considered the springboard for the glories that ensued. We are following in the footsteps of ancestors that bequeathed to us a recipe for healthy eating and cheerful living.

Recognize and trust your "gut instinct":

As our "second brain", we have seen that the third circle of energy boosts the centring of vitality and converts food intake into friendly microbes. It also plays a key role in guiding our everyday thinking and decisions, which we ascribe to our "gut feeling" or "intuition". Nobel laureate and professor of psychology at Princeton University, Daniel Kahneman, distinguishes between "fast" and "slow" thinking. "Fast" thinking (what he terms system 1) is automatic, quick, with an element of cognitive ease, while "slow" thinking or "system 2" is deliberate and controlled. With intuition or "fast" thinking, there is a magical ingredient, "knowing without knowing how we know" (Kahneman). This "magic" underlies some of our most profound and captivating experiences; the Indian philosopher and seer, Osho, affirms that "out of your intuition arises the possibility of art, of aesthetics, of love, of friendship" (Osho 3). We begin to trust this marvellous faculty in generating ideas and sentiments that can move others, as well as in cementing commitments of intimacy that shape our lives in meaningful intensity.

Despite its somewhat "unknowable" genesis, both Kahneman and fellow Nobel laureate Herb Simon ascribe the potency of intuition to **recognition** based on an enormous accumulation of experiences, arising from a sufficiently regular world that provides reinforcement and immediate feedback to our perceptions (Kahneman, Simon). We create coherent narratives from these patterns of experience, driving a subjective confidence in our ability to navigate everyday problems and make sound choices. Of course, our intuitions may be flawed or illusory, relying upon preconceptions and hasty conclusions (Kahneman). However, our capacity for "fast" thinking continues to fascinate and inspire us toward the expression of some of our noblest instincts.

Creativity: Intuition is Central

Frank Denyer, English pianist and composer and winner of the Royal Philharmonic Society's large-scale composition award in 2020 for his work *"The Fish that became the Sun"*, reflects on the role of intuition in his art:

"Speaking for myself, both as a performer and composer, intuition is central. This is because diverse intellectual, physical, aesthetic, sensual and various experiential needs have to be synthesised in real time. They may be pulling in quite different directions but as they have roots below consciousness, intuition is for me the only way to mediate between them and find a path through, although it may be different for other sensibilities. Inspiration is not a something 'beyond', something 'other', but arises from an ongoing engagement with sound and all the many other things that make up life. It is not 'other', just a part of the life I have chosen and in which I am very much engaged" (Denyer).

Intuition: Recognition becomes a spontaneous joy of connection

While the Buddha gifted us a path to overcome everyday struggle and suffering toward equanimity and inner joy, Japanese Zen Buddhism offered the possibility of "*Satori*", a moment of spontaneous and astonishing insight. Zen is rooted in the reverence for nature, a continuation of earlier Japanese belief and practice, and permeated the arts that flowered in that blessed archipelago. The recognition of our intimate links with other forms of life underlies much of Haiku poetry with its rich imagery and flashes of "*Satori*", captured by the incomparable Basho[9]:

When I look carefully
I see the nazunia blooming
by the hedge!

The nazunia is a very ordinary flower, growing easily by the wayside, and easy to overlook when compared to the beauty of other blooms. By turning his complete attention to this humble plant, Basho achieves transcendence: "Rather than possessing the flower, he is possessed by it…if a nazunia can contain such poetry, then each stone can become a sermon" (Osho 177). An intuition of oneness and connectedness completely bypasses the organized and methodical mind, implanted in the beauty of the moment. Observation is complete in itself, with no observer or observed.

Learning Activity – Listening: Shakuhachi (Japanese Bamboo Flute)
"*Shika No Tone*" (*The Distant Call of the Deer*)
Kohachiro Miyata and Rodrigo Rodriguez
https://www.youtube.com/watch?v=7h-dgPfcXH8
November 3, 2018. Accessed 25.1.2021

---

[9]   Matsuo Basho (1644-94) is considered one of the greatest masters of *Haiku* poetry.

The *shakuhachi* shares its history with Zen: the *Fuke* sect of Zen monks used the songs or "*honkyoku*" as a form of "*suizen*" or sound meditation. The songs were adapted to the players' breathing, enabling an ever deeper melding of sound with the inner space of the performer. The monks became known as "*komuso*", the priests of "nothingness" or "emptiness", which are powerful Buddhist concepts of reducing the clutter of the everyday, chattering mind.

Among the most challenging "*honkyoku*" for the *shakuhachi* is the "*Shika No Tone*" or "The Distant Call of the Deer". Haunting and mesmerizing music, played by two contemporary masters, unites an instrument crafted from one of nature's most hardy and pliable creations with an endearing creature of the animal kingdom, and the human quest for communion with both. These sounds emerge from deep within the gut and subside back into the core of silence.

Laughing from the gut: "Life is too important to be taken seriously".

From stillness to uproar, the belly bears witness to diverse dimensions of the human drama. The "hearty laugh" seems a misnomer, since it emerges from deeper in the anatomy, akin to a "jogging for the intestines" (Anderson). Quite appropriately, the "Laughing Buddha" (*Budai* in China, *Kotei* in Japan) sports a weighty paunch. Having absorbed the sufferings and misfortunes of life, his jollity is the gift of tranquillity and contentment. Usually portrayed with the cloth sack of the wanderer, his serenity has little to do with material accumulation; rather, this is an abundance born from the joy of treading lightly upon the earth and discovering humour as the secret ingredient of fulfilment. *Budai* anticipated the words of the supreme comedian of the 20th century, Charlie Chaplin: "a day without laughter is a day wasted".

Humour has accompanied humans from our early discovery that it delivers a "natural high" to our brains, releasing dopamine as comfortably as chocolate. The bonding chemical, oxytocin, surges in shared laughter as much as releasing endorphins, our innate painkillers. The Scientific American confirmed in 1994 that even the precursor to mirth, the Duchenne smile (named after a 19th century French neurologist) generates a neural response that gives our immune system a boost. Studies in California attest that laughter lowers blood pressure, reduces stress hormones, and raises blood levels of T cells, interferon gamma and B cells, which carry anti-cancer properties (Anderson). Chaplin was prescient in advising us to incorporate laughter into our daily routine, completing the trio with diet and exercise in nurturing wellness of body and mind.

Humour and laughter partner with another joyful segment of the brain, the spark of creativity. The associative theory places our ability to create non-obvious connections between seemingly unrelated items in the Posterior Superior Temporal Sulcus (PSTS), the brain's right hemisphere equivalent of Wernicke's area that generates linguistic creativity, processing novel metaphors in poetry and associations between unrelated words (Kudrowitz). The adjacent Anterior STS ignites the "Aha" moment, evident when we get the punchline in a joke. Humour can take many forms, not always positive: initiating emotional release or laughing at the misfortune of others (captured in the German word "Schadenfreude"), even veering into cultural stereotypes. However, it is the incongruity, the unexpected coming together of two things, which often bridges humour and innovation. The fly etched on the urinals at Amsterdam's Schiphol Airport, for example, resulted in 80% less spillage, an effective focusing of errant male behaviour! (Kudrowitz). Improvising comedians hone their skills and thrive on spawning multiple ideas with unpredictable outcomes, the source of spontaneous *"Aha's"* in their audiences.

Learning Activity: Choose Your Humour, Practice Your Laughter

Individual preference can partake of an infinite treasure trove in humour and comedy. There is deep comfort for me to revisit my childhood delight in the playful wit of Oscar Wilde, the hilarious eccentricities of the English upper class in P.G. Wodehouse, the slapstick of Laurel and Hardy, the razor repartee of Groucho Marx, and the piercing humanism of comedy in Chaplin. Globalization and the mingling of diverse tongues and ethnicities provided grist for the levity of *"Mind Your Language"* and the rather more rapier schtick of stand-ups like the Indian Canadian, Russell Peters, in *"Outsourced"*. During the enforced Covid lockdowns, one could continue to revel in Netflix induced oxytocin gaiety with the marvellous Canadian serial *"Schitt's Creek"* and the satire that captured the absurdities of this most odd year in human history, appropriately dubbed *"Death to 2020"*.

Whatever your choice of humour, there is no gainsaying a daily guffaw, especially in the company of other jest-niks. Laughter Clubs have sprung up in Indian cities, adding a pleasing counterpoint to their clamorous cacophony. For those reluctant to stretch their limbs with a morning run, here is a good alternative in a salubrious jog for the intestines!

Learning Activity: 100 Laughter Yoga Exercises
https://www.youtube.com/watch?v=Fq4kTZuLops
June 16, 2013. Accessed 2.2.2021.

This video offers an entire workout session with a variety of laughter exercises, collected from different parts of the world, releasing the funny bones and endorphins in equal measure. (Warning: it is highly contagious!).

Regardless of the stimulus, remember to smile and light the room, laugh and light the world.

The Navels of the World: Radiating Centres of Excellence and Fulfilment

Long before the discovery of the "gut-brain axis", our remarkable civilizations intuited the core of their achievements and wisdom emanating from a metaphorical "navel". The locus of the umbilical cord generated the vitality and the binding threads that inspired countless generations and continue to reverberate in our times. We are fortunate in the opportunity to witness these masterpieces of human endeavour for ourselves, eternal beacons of illumination.

Benares: the City of Eternal Light and Liberation

Rising from the banks of the River Ganga (Ganges) in Northern India, Benares is one of the oldest inhabited cities in the world and seems as antique as time itself. In his journey around the globe, Mark Twain mused that "Benares is older than history, older than tradition, older even than legend, and looks twice as old as all of them put together!" As a contemporary traveller makes her way through the narrow lanes and alleyways, elbowed by rickshaws, cows, swarms of humanity and assaulted by scents of every conceivable variety arising from the hoary walls, she is indeed in the presence of a place unlike any other in existence. For Benares is the navel of an entire cosmology, "a living text of Hinduism" (Eck 6), the ageless and endless destination of pilgrims from every corner of India and beyond: "The India that we see here reflects the elaborate and ancient ritual tradition of Hinduism. It is a tradition of pilgrimage to sacred places, bathing in sacred waters, and honouring divine images…It is a tradition that has imagined and imaged God in a thousand ways…It is a religious tradition that understands life and death as an integrated whole" (6). Count Hermann Keyserling, a 19th century Prussian traveller, gushed that "Benares is holy. Europe, grown superficial, hardly understands such truths anymore…**I feel nearer here than I have ever done to the heart of the world**; here I feel everyday as if soon, perhaps even today, I would receive the grace of supreme revelation". (in Eck 17)

Despite the throbbing intensity of daily activity here, the antiquity and spiritual significance of Benares give it an other-worldly ambience. It may feel like the centre of the world, as experienced by Count Keyserling, but it is also detached from the earth, sitting atop the trident of its lord and protector, the Hindu god *Shiva* and "not subject to the relentless movement of the great cycles of time…it is the still centre which anchors the perpetual movement of time and space". (Eck 24) Benares is the unmoving witness of the human spectacle, yet also its shining inspiration, explaining its first and popular name for Hindus: *Kashi* or the City of Light. Today it is more commonly called by another ancient name, *Varanasi*, derived probably from the rivers *Varana* and *Asi* that flow into the Ganga from different directions and create a sacred confluence in the city. "*Baranasi*" was the version in the Pali language, corrupted later to "*Banaras*" or "*Benares*". This is an appropriate tribute to the Buddha, who preached his first sermon in Pali at Sarnath, close to Benares, adding another intense spiritual vibration to this hallowed land. Yet, the reigning energy at *Varanasi* belongs to "*Sada Shiva*" , the Eternal Lord Shiva.

The genius of Hindu thought and civilization is the ability to meld multiplicity and unity in a dazzling synthesis. By some counts, 330 million deities are worshipped in diverse corners of the country with an astonishing array of rituals and practices, yet they are considered emanations of one supreme spiritual principle or "*Brahman*". A trinity of *Brahma* (Creator), *Vishnu* (Sustainer) and *Shiva* (Destroyer) represent the three integral elements of "*Brahman*", each completed by their female counterparts. Yet, those who worship *Shiva* view him as the unifier of all elements. In him, creation and dissolution merge and he "challenges ordinary distinctions of pure and impure, auspicious and inauspicious" (33) . In his form as "*Ardhanarishvara*", the divergence of male and female melts in biological fusion. Ambiguities are often the lifeblood of human existence, but here they coalesce in celebration of a cosmic pulse. Even that implacable opposition of life and death dissolves in Benares. The pollution of death is rendered holy on the banks of the sacred river as cremation fires jostle with morning and evening prayers and incantations from the "*ghats*" (landings) and temples. To die in Benares is to find liberation from "*Samsara*", the endless trap of birth and demise, toward celestial bliss.

The sacred geography of Benares attracted pilgrims throughout the aeons, and modern tourists mingle with them in a pleasing bond of fellow wanderers. As the god *Indra* promised, travel is liberation too. He urged the life of the road upon a young man named Rohita: "***There is no happiness for him who does not travel***, *Rohita. Living in the society of men, the best man becomes a sinner... Therefore, wander! The feet of the wanderer are like the flower, his soul is growing and reaping the fruit. Therefore, wander! The fortune of him who is sitting, sits; it rises when he rises; it sleeps when he sleeps; it moves when he moves. Therefore, wander!*"[10] While most pilgrims yearn for the "*darshana*" or sacred sight-seeing of their deity, as a traveller and photographer I am afforded the "*darshana*" of the most incredible assortment of people and sights that one could hope to encounter on this planet. Benares lives up to yet another of its names, "The Forest of Bliss".

"Older than history, older than legend"

---

[10] Eck (21). Indra is the protector of travellers.

Solitary liberation

Pilgrim

The final journey (cremation at the Ganga)

Benares photographs (credit: author).

Xi'an: The Springboard of Long Peace and Infinite Exchange

Human flourishing through the ages has relied upon an expansion of interaction and sharing across often daunting frontiers. The Chinese term *"Tai"* celebrates periods when communication between individuals across the world is open and people are receptive to new ideas and things. This was the spirit that propelled the incredible cross-cultural contact along the Silk Road for over a thousand years, bridging the riches and achievements of Chinese civilizations with those of South and West Asia and Mediterranean Europe. Braving the treacherous terrain of deserts, mountains, swamps and brigand raids, a steady stream of traders, adventurers, artists, preachers and pilgrims exchanged their goods, beliefs, fashion, and stories in a remarkable foretaste of our own era of global networking.

The Silk Road stretched from *Chang'an* (modern *Xi'an*), the capital of the golden *T'ang* dynasty of China, to the centre of European opulence at Rome. *Chang'an* translates appropriately as "Long Peace", the fulcrum of a sophisticated and enduring civilization based on the stability of imperial rule. In their sustained history, the Chinese were ruled just once by an Empress, *Wu Zetian* (lived 642-705 CE, reigned 660-705 CE). In the following extract from *Empress: A Novel*, author Shan Sa recreates the splendour of *Chang'an* and the exultation of Empress Wu at the renown and cosmopolitan flavour of her city:

"To encourage households all over China, I set an example by rearing silk worms in the imperial parks. Caravans came from the west in search of porcelain and silk, breathing new life into our civilization. Our women, tired of being swaddled in several layers of dresses with long sleeves, now chose tunics with narrow sleeves, wide trousers, and leather boots that freed their feet from the constraints of rigid shoes with curled toes. The dizzying height of our traditional headdresses required hours of work, and they were so heavy that they impaired our movements. The desert women wore their hair simply dressed, crowned with light felt hats; by imitating them, we could walk or run as fast as men.

The craze for foreign foods and exotic spices kept expanding. Furniture from western kingdoms streamed into China, piled on camels' backs. High-level chairs and tables and raised beds allowed us to stretch our legs and brought beneficial comforts to our everyday lives. The music from the oasis conquered us with its powerful impulsive rhythms. The twirling dances from those parts- so different from the Chinese dances that included restricted and graceful slowness and ritual gestures — showed us all the beauty of spontaneity.

Imperial patrols guaranteed the safety of the Silk Road through the Gobi desert. Inside the Great Wall, new inns had been made to make the journey easier for travellers. In Long Peace, I opened academies to provide a forum for foreign scholars and Chinese tutors to pass on their knowledge, train interpreters, and compile dictionaries in every language.

Officials complained about the growing number of temples dedicated to unknown idols, but I ignored these pointless concerns. Buddha was a god who had been revealed to the West, and the spread of the Buddhist faith had never eclipsed the glory of the deities we had venerated since the dawn of time. Every religion was a blade that allowed its faithful to carve up the lie that is life. I encouraged my people to choose the tool that suited them best.

In my eyes, a country's enthusiasm for other customs was the mark of a great civilization that could absorb every difference. *This new wealth and the abundance of our own ancient heritage had transformed China into a stellar empire that shone beyond its own borders. Distant kingdoms dreamed of Long Peace as a city destined to be happy and prosperous. Our criteria for elegance became the universal points of reference for good taste. Western kings and far-eastern princes sent their scholars to our Court to study politics, justice, administration, military organization, medicine, literature, the arts, and architecture. Numerous foreign capitals took their inspiration from the example set by Long Peace, and their imperial palaces were smaller copies of ours. Chinese was the most widespread language in the world, and it became the official language of diplomacy with which every kingdom could communicate. The morals and ethics of Confucius were adopted by many countries and served as a code of behaviour and an official doctrine"* (Shan Sa 157-159*).*

Tourists flocking to *Xi'an* today are drawn primarily to the astonishing durability and artistic virtuosity of the Terracotta Warriors, which predate the *T'ang* dynasty by six centuries. For me, though, the description of *Chang'an* in the reign of Empress Wu carries greater resonance with the resurgence of contemporary China, particularly its revived trust in global exchange and connectedness, contributing to the prosperity and edification of citizens everywhere.

Delphi: The Prophecy of Deep Thought and Beauty

On the slopes of Mount Parnassus in Central Greece, at the meeting point of two eagles sent forth by Zeus[11] and amidst the hallucinogenic vapours spewing from a geological fault line, the Temple of Apollo at Delphi became the "omphalos"[12] of a civilization that continues to inspire the Western world and, by extension, all of humanity. Rulers, citizens, and pilgrims from diverse parts of Greece and beyond trekked to decipher their fate and solicit advice from the Oracle at the temple, a priestess whose cryptic messages carried the imprint of the fumes of ethylene emanating from the magical earth. Her utterances elevated the aura and intensity of truths emerging from a trance-like clarity. They created the abiding legacy of Delphi as the heart of a daring exploration and fulfilment of the human mind: "curious, innovative, critical, intensely engaged with life and with death, searching for order and meaning yet sceptical of conventional verities, the Greeks were originators of intellectual values as relevant today as they were in the 5th century BCE" (Tarnas 2).

Amongst the most prophetic and profound pronouncements of the Oracle was to declare that no man was wiser than the philosopher, Socrates. The seed of his thoughts, developed and amplified by his successors, Plato and Aristotle, became the radiant flowers of deep inquiry and discernment. Socrates is honoured at Delphi with his abiding dictum inscribed on its walls: "Know thyself". The Oracle divined that, far from an egotistic tenet, this insight flowed from Socrates' awareness of his own ignorance and his passion for the pursuit of truth; "not as the creed of an introspective subjectivist, but as a directive to universal understanding" (47). In remarkable unison with his contemporary, the Buddha, Socrates declared the mind as the central force in life and its awakening, an avenue open to all. Reasoning through dialogue or "the dialectical argument" became the basis for the "Socratic method" , a lifelong quest for

---

[11] The supreme Greek god in a polytheistic belief system.
[12] Greek for "bellybutton" or the navel

critical self-reflection and enhancing learning for others: "Socrates often referred to himself as an intellectual midwife, through his dialectical skill bringing to birth the latent truth in another's mind" (34). He embodied rationality and morality, wisdom and goodness, as well as the courage to accept the ultimate punishment for his convictions.

Plato extended the vision of his teacher, Socrates, in uniting the ethical and the rational with the aesthetic: the Good, the True, and the Beautiful merged in the realm of a supreme Ideal, which could be intuited by the mind. For Plato, ideas were superior to the concrete world revealed by our senses, best exemplified in the perfect and changeless notions of number and geometry in mathematics, an underlying order and beauty in the Cosmos and a celestial music. The philosophical vision required the temperament of a lover, allowing oneself "to be inwardly grasped by the most sublime force of Eros – that universal passion to restore a former unity, to overcome the separation from the divine and become one with it" (41). Plato's mystical perception found echoes in the intense poetry, song, and dance of the Sufi Islamic orders in their quest for divine love more than a millennium later. In our own age, beset by the deluge of competing claims from multiple sources, the Allegory of the Cave[13] remains a powerful lesson in sifting the authentic knowledge of reality from the illusion of appearances and shadows in the guise of misinformation and blatant mis-truths. Plato's "light" that attempts to redeem the occupants of the cave has never seemed more pertinent.

In keeping with the Greek tradition of critical inquiry, Plato's student, Aristotle, questioned his teacher's idealism. The empirical world of concrete objects, examined with a trust in our sensory perception, was to Aristotle the true reality rather than an imperceptible world of eternal

---

13 The allegory describes a group of people chained to the wall of a cave, who perceive the shadows cast on the wall by a fire as "reality", although these are illusions and not truthful representations. An outsider (the philosopher) attempts to bring the light of truth to the cave dwellers, but they remain tied to their prison.

ideas. While Plato found his ideal in abstract mathematics, Aristotle favoured the science of organic biology, in which each organism moved from a state of potentiality to its realized form in actuality. Change and movement were inherent in the idea of potentiality, and we may discern here the kernel of Darwin's theory of the evolution of species that would transform our thinking many centuries later. Aristotle linked the dynamic character of organisms perceived by our senses, to the nature of the human mind itself, an active intellect (nous) that gave us "the intuitive capacity to grasp final and universal truths"[14] (60). However, Aristotle's more empirical and pragmatic outlook also led to the realization that universal and absolute knowledge could not be attained in all areas.

Morality and ethics, for instance, was in "the realm of the contingent", dependent on varying contexts and requiring practical solutions to specific problems (67). This insight informs the notion of "relativity" in ethics, whose aim is not to arrive at an understanding of "absolute virtue" but to cradle the emergence of a virtuous person in their own milieu.[15]

Plato's ideal of the Beautiful was extended and modified by Aristotle's greater attention to the physical and natural world as apprehended by the senses, leading to a celebration of the human body that was unsurpassed elsewhere. Whether in athletic skill, personal beauty, or artistic creation, the body became central in the expression of Greek flair and accomplishment. Delphi staged the Pythian games, a regular athletic festival with running, boxing, wrestling and chariot racing, that rivalled the Olympics. The participants were inspired by artistic masterpieces displayed around the temple, as much as artists through the ages who

---

[14] In both Plato and Aristotle, we see the trust in the interaction of rational and intuitive thought, which Daniel Kahneman has termed "slow" and "fast" thinking, discussed on page 82 in this chapter.

[15] This tension underlies the Declaration of the Universal Human Rights by the United Nations since its founding in 1945, and the complexities of its implementation and interpretation in different cultural and political contexts.

have sought to imitate or exceed the golden proportions displayed in sculpture, frieze, mural or painting. None more so than the geniuses of the Italian Renaissance, conscious inheritors of the Greek legacy.

One of the Renaissance greats, Raphael, embodied the contrasting visions of Plato and Aristotle in his exquisite piece, *The School of Athens*. At the focal spot of the painting, Plato points heavenward in his search for the Ideal Form, while Aristotle gestures toward the earth in the quest of perceiving concrete reality. The ambience is far from discord, rather an amiable realization of the diversity of paths in the inquiring mind leading to a pleasing synthesis of knowledge and wisdom.

Raphael: *School of Athens* (detail).[16]

---

[16] Image source: *christopherpjones.medium.com* (accessed: 20.12.2020)

The picture includes several other philosophers and artists, **upholding the Greek affirmation of the plurality of human faculties and thought, each contributing their stream to enhanced understanding through the ages.** They would include the Humanists such as Protagoras, who boldly proclaimed that individual judgements should form the basis of one's personal belief and conduct rather than conforming to traditional religious or conventional dogma. The Epicureans asserted the central value of human pleasure, overcoming fear of the gods and death, best achieved in the company of friends. Despite the multiplicity of perspectives, the Greeks intuited "a sense of the universe as an ordered whole, a cosmos rather than a chaos" (17). The temple at Delphi appropriately worshipped Apollo, the god of order and harmony. Plato fulfilled his teacher's vision of *"Kosmos"*, "a peculiarly Greek combination of order, structural perfection, and beauty...as restated by Plato, to discover *kosmos* in the world was to reveal *kosmos* in one's own soul" (47). This was truly to "know thyself", as Socrates had exhorted, and Delphi has preserved for eternity.

Yogyakarta (Jogja): The Confluence of Faith, Tolerance and Etiquette

Nurtured by the fertile and lush soil of Central Java in Indonesia, Yogyakarta (popularly known as Jogja) became the epicentre of the most remarkable synthesis of beliefs and practices. Ringed by volcanic mountains and the sea, one can observe the worship of nature, originating from the earliest animist faith, in the sacred rice mound or *"tumpeng"* that graces every celebratory meal here. Within an hour, the wanderer can marvel at the exquisite setting and inspiring ascent to the gate of enlightenment at the Borobudur, the grandest Buddhist monument in the world. Back in Jogja, arise the magnificent spires of the Prambanan temple dedicated to the Hindu trinity of Brahma, Wisnu and Siwa[17].

---

[17] *Wisnu* and *Siwa* are the Indonesian terms for *Vishnu* (the Preserver) and *Shiva* (the Destroyer) in Indian Hindu belief. *Brahma* (the Creator) is constant.

At the universities and other centres of learning, we may partake of the wisdom of Islamic teaching from the holy Qu'ran and the Hadith (the pronouncements of the Prophet). All roads converge, though, at the *Keraton* or Palace at Jogja, which set the tone for centuries of "*halus*" or refined and courteous etiquette for Javanese and Indonesians. Moved by my visit to this exquisite jewel, I remarked that "in my study of world civilizations, I have never come across any mental construct as sophisticated and tolerant as the multiple, dynamic frameworks of Javanese thought, **the perfect model for our globalizing world**" (Bammi 113).

The architecture at Jogja propels the viewer into a stunning array of revelations. The Borobudur, designed to replicate a "cosmic mandala", symbolizes the ascent of the soul from ignorance and misery to the liberation of joyful contentment, conveyed in exquisite sculptural detail. At its base, the pilgrim confronts the realm of *Kamadhatu*, the desires and entrapments of ordinary and universal human suffering. At the *Rupadhatu* (realm of form), we are edified and instructed by the stories of the Buddha and the *Bodhisattvas*[18], their compassion engulfing the sorrows and struggles of all living beings and indicating the path toward a different and exalted outlook. Seated in meditative calm on one of the panels here, we can sense the Buddha's confidence as he proclaims: "Let me tell you what I lost through meditation – sickness, anger, depression, insecurity, the burden of old age, the fear of death"[19]. This air of serenity permeates the upper level at Borobudur, the square terraces transforming into a circular array of *stupas*[20], the shapes and signs of completion. We are now in *Arupadhatu*, the formless realm, which preserves the eternal wisdom of the Buddha. Appropriately, though, some images of the Great

---

[18] *Boddhisattvas* are enlightened and compassionate beings who continue to exist in our midst to assist our journey away from anguish and tribulation.

[19] From the "*Dhammapada*" ("The Path of the Universal Law")

[20] *Stupas* are mound-shaped structures that contain sacred relics and the wisdom of the Buddha.

Liberator escaped the confines of the *stupas*, creating a magnificent symphonic pinnacle with a neighbouring mountaintop.

The Prambanan temple arose from a typically Indonesian fusion of local and imported narratives. Although this 9ᵗʰ century CE masterpiece celebrates Lord *Siwa*, the Hindu god of destruction, legend grants greater prominence to the Javanese princess *Loro Jonggrang*. Sought in marriage by the prince who had murdered her father, she set the condition that he would have to construct a thousand temples in one night. With the help of the spirits, this task appeared to be near completion, but *Loro Jonggrang* bewitched the roosters into declaring an early dawn, and the spirits disappeared at 999. In fury, the prince struck her down, but Lord

Siwa converted her into the stone idol of his wife, *Durga*, an icon of worship ever since. In a further act of generosity, *Siwa* permitted the builders of Prambanan to raise their fluted towers of brilliance to his partners in the Hindu trinity – *Brahma* and *Wisnu* – and to enjoy the companionship of their consorts, *Saraswati* (goddess of learning and wisdom) and *Laksmi* (goddess of prosperity), respectively. The animist element was not far behind, with sculpted pavilions dedicated to the favourite animals of the Trinity – *Brahma's Hamsa* (swan), *Wisnu's Garuda* (eagle), and *Siwa's Nandi* (bull). Today, the Prambanan has become the spectacular backdrop for a performance of the *Ramayana* dance drama. Incredibly, the world's largest Islamic country, Indonesia, has adopted the *Garuda* as its national symbol and its most popular traditional entertainment, the *Wayang* puppet theatre, celebrates the stories of the *Ramayana* and *Mahabharata* epics of Indian Hindu origin!

The *Wayang* was nurtured in the genteel and aristocratic ambience of the Javanese courts at Jogja and its neighbour, Surakarta (Solo). Here again we inhabit a world of plurality and multiplicity, of intricate and overlapping layers, skilfully orchestrated by the *Dhalang* (puppet master). The audiences for these timeless tales include the gods, ancestor heroes, nature, and the clowns (us, the ordinary living folk), addressed in languages ranging from Sanskrit and classical Javanese to Indonesian and American English. The flexible format enables the *Dhalang* to weave in stories of *Wali* saints who popularized Islam in Java with Hindu and Buddhist themes, as well as modern messages of national purpose. The etiquette of Javanese behaviour is reinforced as well, contrasting the notions of "*halus*" (refined) and "*kasar*" (crude) with expressions such as "*adol gendhung*" warning against impolite, boastful, or disrespectful action and enjoining the virtues of Princess *Sembadra*, "whose words and actions are as sweet as sugar water". Even, or most especially, the *Sultan* (ruler) must live up to the norms of "*halus*". At the confluence of five streets leading to the palace gate, he is inspired to concentrate the senses and the mind on the worship of the higher Almighty, and at the fragrant *tlampok* tree he is reminded of the Javanese perfume of goodness: "speak always nicely, so your name will be famous all over the world". The fragrance of soft speech, respect, and civility has indeed radiated across this charming and mellow land and its people.

Listening Activity: The Javanese Gamelan

The Sultan's Pleasure – Javanese Gamelan and vocal music from the palace of Yogyakarta (1986)
www.youtube.com/watch?v=CxeJxAUlhxA&t=185s
April 18, 2018. Accessed: 15.2.2021

In contrast to the lively and brisk tempo of the *gamelan* orchestra from Bali (introduced on pages 69-70 in the "Second Circle"), the Javanese *gamelan* creates a calm and meditative vibration. We are fortunate to listen to a recording from the palace at Yogyakarta, where the instruments of the *gamelan* and the dulcet tones of the *"Sindhen"* female singers combine in a mystical and soothing ambience, another strand in the *"halus"* refinement at the court. This music is the perfect overture to the rising Slow Movement in other corners of the globe today.

The Emerging "Navels" of Tomorrow: Slow Cities, Slow Living, Slow Travel

Many ills of our times could be traced to the dramatic increase in the pace of life which accompanied the growth of an industrial civilization and the more recent onset of the era of the internet, social media, and automation. The combined assault of fast transport, fast work, fast machines, fast food and fast learning seems to have siphoned away the joy of living for so many. Fortunately, human ingenuity and resilience did not disappear altogether, and we see the emergence of a movement since the 1980's to restore a more leisurely and unrushed tempo of existence. Appropriately, the birth of this "andante"[21] rhythm began in the smaller cities of Italy[22], where *Citta Slow* (Slow Cities) were twinned with Slow Food, an outflow of the Mediterranean penchant for elegant living. Much of the appeal and relevance of the movement stems from the attempt to preserve local traditions and systems combined with the urgent need for global ecological awareness. In a manifesto that would please Epicureans of all ages, one of the key tenets of Slow Food is the belief in the right to pleasure: "A firm defence of quiet material pleasure is the only way to oppose the universal folly of Fast Life" (*Footprint*). This includes conserving cultural cuisine, food plants and seeds, cattle and farming practices of an ecoregion. As we discovered earlier, good eating in this part of the world sustains strong social ties: "the pleasures of food preparation and consumption among friends and family helps develop social and cultural capital" (*Footprint*).

The beliefs of *Citta Slow* and Slow Food are being emulated (slowly, of course) in other parts of the world, with the ripple effect reaching into multiple dimensions. Slow Books promises us a return to the delights of reading, with the accompanying soaring of the imagination and expansion of the mind as we encounter different realities. Slow Schools would reorient our learning further, away from the obsession with standardized testing and outcomes toward the process of discovery and meaningful relationships. As part of "ecological literacy", school yards involve students in planting, tending, and harvesting plants, with a natural extension in urban farming in their adult lives[23]. Here we are sowing the seeds of a deeper bond with the soil and the community, which we can experience for ourselves in Slow Travel. Rather than the hectic "sightseeing"

---

21 In music, "andante" denotes a moderate tempo, akin to a leisurely walk or stroll.

22 Limited to cities with populations up to 50,000, though some of their practices could be transferable to our big or even mega cities.

23 A learning activity with a similar "existential dimension" and "planet-centered" approach was introduced on pages 24-25 in the "first circle".

of modern tourism, this is an opportunity to immerse with local people, life, and culture and consider imparting skills to others in "voluntourism". We may be on the way to recreating the unhurried pathways of exchange from the ancient Silk Road, without most of the attendant hazards!

Apart from the desire to create more humane living spaces, the appearing "navels" of our age encourage an attitude of mindful living and the re-birth of our inherited sources of joy: good food and drink, association with others, wandering with a sedate stride, and inventive effort. Above all, it is an attempt to reclaim that most precious gift – time itself.

Sources/Citations

Anderson, Gene. "Humour and Health" (TedX Bay City).
www.youtube.com/watch?v=4BcnAKBju3w&t=601s
February 15, 2016.

Bammi, Vivek. 2005. *Indonesia: A Feast for the Senses.* Jakarta, PT Sukarya and Sukarya.

Corcos, Daniel. *"Exercise and the Brain".*
https://www.youtube.com/watch?v=8ItYlTc6LiU
February 2, 2017.

Denyer, Frank. *Personal communication with the author.*
October 28, 2020.

Eck, Diana L. 1982. *Banaras: City of Light.* New York, Alfred A. Knopf

Footprint Choices. 2021. *"Slow Movement".* Web: https://www.slowmovement.com/slow_living.php
Accessed: 7.2.2021

Kahneman, Daniel. "Thinking, Fast and Slow" (Google).
https://www.youtube.com/watch?v=CjVQJdIrDJ0&t=19s

November 11, 2011.

Knight, Rob. *"Follow your gut; microbiomes and aging"*.
https://www.youtube.com/watch?v=2iKHMyWzclM
March 6, 2017.

Kramer, Art. *"Exercise and the Brain Symposium"*.
https://www.youtube.com/watch?v=uy1-SSPU4IM
October 16, 2014.

Kudrowitz, Barry. *"How humour can fuel innovation"*.
www.youtube.com/watch?v=Vl3v0Q0eYQ4&t=326s
June 27, 2014.

Mannino, Michael. *"The Moving Mind: Neuroscience, Philosophy, and Fitness"*.
https://www.youtube.com/watch?v=nQH6CQ_qqY0
August 31, 2017.

Metzl, Jordan. *"The Exercise Cure"* (Google).
www.youtube.com/watch?v=N8ckQR7KCCs&t=1677s
April 1, 2014.

Mosconi, Lisa and Kwik, Jim. *"Eating for your brain with Dr. Lisa Mosconi"*. (Kwik Brain Episode 88).
www.youtube.com/watch?v=qxiAmJllp4I&t=1180s
December 15, 2018.

Naidoo, Uma. *"This is your brain on food"*. (Brain Warrior's podcast).
https://www.youtube.com/watch?v=9FxOvU2rdC4
July 27, 2020.

Osho. 2001. *Intuition: Knowing Beyond Logic*. New York, St. Martin's Griffin.

Pascual-Leone, Alvaro. *"How to keep your brain healthy through exercise"*.

https://www.youtube.com/watch?v=VUSIVuXiWUo&t=1s
May 16, 2016.

Ratey, John J. *"Run, Jump, Learn! How Exercise can Transform our Schools"*.
https://www.youtube.com/watch?v=hBSVZdTQmDs
November 19, 2012.

Rossi, Megan. *"Gut health – the secret to happiness?"*
www.youtube.com/watch?v=OGRRkuKY7sA&t=1371s
June 10, 2020.

Shan Sa. 2006. *Empress: A Novel.* New York, Harper Collins.

Spector, Tim. *"What role does our microbiome play in a healthy diet?"*
https://www.youtube.com/watch?v=-LUuqxQSaFQ
February 27, 2019.

Suzuki, Wendy. *"The brain-changing benefits of exercise"*.
https://www.youtube.com/watch?v=BHY0FxzoKZE
March 21, 2018.

Tarnas, Richard. 1991. *The Passion of the Western Mind.* New York,
Ballantine Books.

The Fourth Circle of Joy

Midway in our journey, we arrive at the central juncture. The heart is not just the core of our biological being, but also the arena for the dramatic play of passions and sentiments that shape our interactions with others and the self. Harnessing the energy of emotions makes this the most challenging and decisive circle in the adventure to fulfil our deepest aspirations. We must confront the universal reality of adversity and its impact on physical and mental wellbeing. Negative and destructive emotions cannot be ignored, especially as we witness their devastating footprint throughout human history and the ominous shadows they continue to cast on individuals and societies today. Through careful attention and skilful effort, though, we can transform the quality of our responses and channel constructive vitality to the higher circles.

Fortunately, we can rely upon a fruitful partnership between wisdom traditions and contemporary science. Buddhism combines an unblinking observation of human suffering and negative mind states with pragmatic understanding and practices that move us toward a purposeful engagement with the world. Neuroscience confirms that our brain is dynamic, adaptable and flexible, an agent of change and boundless learning. The common features in these perspectives creates trust in a **developmental process**. We look at two curricular paths integrating a similar approach: Social, Emotional, Ethical Learning includes a specific focus on ethical values and practices that enhance active participation and belonging to communities beyond the self; the Growth Mindset establishes a paradigm for lifelong learning by confronting challenge and failure as possibilities for rewarding maturation. **We are encouraged to move** from the "small self", mired in daily anxieties, to an expansive mind state, or what philosopher, Andy Clark, calls the "extended mind"[24]. Reflection and awareness are key elements in this flowering, allied to critical thinking that engages with diverse perspectives and openness to re-examining our assumptions. As the Tibetans remind us, healthy and positive emotions emerge from insightful thought and responsible action.

The thread of **connectedness** continues to weave its alchemy in this circle. Civilizations from diverse parts of the world have gifted us the "happiness gene", from which we can benefit generously. Beginning with establishing comfort in one's own emotional moorings, we are invited to strengthen our bonds with ever widening circles of affection and celebration. We may even follow in the footsteps of a nation which commits to happiness as a cultural imperative.

Emotional stability, equanimity and passion become fruitful foundations for the creative outpouring in the ascending circles of energy. We get a foretaste with three joyful musical masterpieces to round off and enliven the heart centre.

Negative and Destructive Emotions: The Root of Unskilful and Unhealthy Actions and Living

Amongst the wisdom traditions of the world, perhaps none has probed the realm of human emotion or feeling[25] with the depth of Tibetan culture. This could perhaps be attributed to its location at the "Roof of the World", amidst the towering Himalayan peaks and valleys, the rarefied air contributing to an intense and focused contemplation on the human condition. It could also have resulted from the historical synthesis of

---

24   For a good read on Andy Clark, see Larissa MacFarquhar's "The Mind-Expanding Ideas of Andy Clark" in *The New Yorker* (April 2, 2018).

25   There is no word in Tibetan that translates directly as the English "emotion"; instead, His Holiness the Dalai Lama clarifies that "feeling is one of five omnipresent mental factors, and the one that is closest to being translatable as emotion" (in Goleman 86).

ancestral Bon and imported Buddhist teachings[26], both emphasizing the role of skilful thought in constructing the foundations of a contented and fulfilled existence, and the centrality of emotional states in the human drama[27]. The dialectic began by uncovering the roots and impact of negative or destructive emotions, so that we could create the journey toward a positive outcome. In their fervent search for understanding, the Tibetans revealed a plethora of adverse emotional states, numbering in the thousands. They became aware that our everyday lives revolve around fairly ordinary emotions, oscillating between "irritation, boredom, impatience, mild amusement, transient frustration, resignation, apprehension, nostalgia, chagrin, contentment, affection, slight feelings of envy, and vague dissatisfaction" (Richards 19). However, by turning the spotlight on some paramount states of negativity, we could focus on a path to improvement in thought and action, with beneficial effects in multiple dimensions.

Using the graphic metaphor of "**thought pollution**", the Tibetans identified eight elements of "mental toxic waste": envy, jealousy, greed, anger, lust, arrogance, careless actions and thoughts, and selfishness (Hansard 21-22). With the Buddhist outlook of compassion and inherent goodness in humans, these "pollutants" are not viewed as tainted with individual guilt or sin, rather as teachers of experience: "they must not be denied but understood, loved and transformed" (22).

Envy and jealousy overlap, but while envy is usually "calculating and brooding", jealousy "is a moment of passionate, untamed, raw desire that someone has something that you do not...like having temporary blindness" (24). The toxic nature of jealousy is brilliantly explored in

---

[26] Buddhism arrived in Tibet from India more than 1200 years ago, while the Bon tradition dates back 17,000 years (Hansard 2).

[27] Modern neuroscience has validated the association between rational thought and attention, located at the brain's prefrontal cortex, and primordial emotions, located at the amygdala, with the hippocampus (memory centre) playing the role of connector.

the English playwright Shakespeare's masterpiece *"Othello"*, where Iago plots the destruction of Othello and his wife Desdemona. In an ironic line from the play, Iago warns Othello *"O, beware, my lord, of jealousy; It is the green-ey'd monster, which doth mock the meat it feeds on."* We may credit Shakespeare with the expression "green with jealousy", which aptly conveys the impact of a deadly poisoning of the insides, sickening the mind and body.

A similar erosion of wellness arises from greed, which ranges from food and wealth to power and ambition without a restraining impulse. Anger, too, may be unrestrained but carries the imprint of an eruption, with palpable consequences on the individual's anatomy and quality of inter-action with others. A study with a group of 20,000 factory workers by Dr. Redford Williams at Duke University in the U.S. concluded that chron-ically angry persons (measured by their levels of hostility) were more likely to die from causes such as heart disease, cancer, and even accidents, over a period of 25 years (Goleman 36). This confirms the Tibetan belief in the strong links between emotion and health, both mental and physical.

Insecurity often seeds noxious sentiments. Anger could emerge from a sense of powerlessness, while lust is an attempt to gain control over others and create self-centred experiences. Arrogance conceals a lack of confi-dence, creating a defensive ring to prevent engagement on equal terms with others. Careless thoughts and actions generate intentional harm on others[28]. Conversely, selfishness is an addictive attitude that "affects the (individual) chemistry of the brain and the body's limbic system, both of which are intimately connected to our emotions" (Hansard 28).

Learning Activity: Reflections on Negative Emotions (for all ages)

The Buddha placed the onus of wellbeing squarely upon each individ-ual, rather than any "greater force" like divinity or Fate. As Buddhadasa

---

[28] These could include "being spiteful, hurting another person or passing on gossip" (Hansard 28).

Kirtisinghe explains, "Happiness and misery, which are the common lot of all living things, especially that of humanity, are not, from a Buddhist point of view, rewards or punishments assigned by a God to a soul that has done good or evil. Buddhists believe in a natural law, called 'cause and effect', common to all worldly phenomena" (*in* Singh 100). Uncovering the cause of negative or destructive emotions implies examining them with clarity and mapping out a path toward positive outcomes. For Tibetans and all Buddhists, "thinking well means taking control of your life" (Hansard 29).

In this learning activity, we choose four or five emotions that are of particular concern to the individual. These could be the "ordinary, everyday" feelings indicated on page 111, or the more significant elements of "thought pollution" discussed above. For young children and teenagers, they may include instances of bullying (both physical and cyber) or exclusion, part of what are labelled by psychologists as acts of "microaggression".

In a journal or blog, identify the sources and impacts of the emotions, observing each one closely. You could refer to specific incidents and persons involved, or more general impressions. Then, consider a scenario in which these negative feelings have begun to fade away, either through your actions or through the realization that emotions, like other phenomena, are not permanent but rather rise and fall (the word itself originates in "motion" or "moving"). Use the power of thought energy to change your perception and to take personal responsibility for more positive interactions with others.

This activity can be repeated at regular periods to fortify the beneficial aspects of reflection, refining the skill of observation and enabling a distance from the tumult of everyday reality. When participants become more comfortable, these observations could spark group discussion and dialogue to enhance mutual learning. As the Tibetans say, emotions may be considered our "teachers of experience".

The nadir of the human saga: hatred and despair

"Thought pollution" can sometimes take on the character of a catastrophic contamination of the human soul, resulting in physical and mental destruction. Hatred builds upon an explosive cocktail of anger, greed, arrogance, and envy, with deadly outcomes. Our history is strewn with examples of thoughts and actions laced with hatred, culminating in horrifying massacres and genocides. At a more familiar and everyday level, many individuals struggle with feelings of anguish and despair, often resulting in depression and suicidal tendencies. What seems to bind hatred and despair is the primal human emotion of **fear,** arising from deep within the primitive or 'reptilian' part of the brain, the amygdala. A hydra-headed entity, fear, too, surfaces in multiple guises with visages of insecurity and the inability to create harmonious relationships with others. As we practiced in the previous learning activity, we must observe these destructive habits with attention and care, on the path to a more beneficial and skilful engagement with reality. We will use the faculties of listening and viewing to consider the impact of these emotions on the self and others.

Listening Activity: Henryk Gorecki Symphony no. 3, "Symphony of Sorrowful Songs"
Dawn Upshaw (soprano) and the London Sinfonietta
https://www.youtube.com/watch?v=87DJF1_vwQA
July 20, 2019. Accessed: 25.2.2021

All three movements of this symphony by the Polish composer, Gorecki, are slow and haunting meditations on loss at its most painful, the separation of parent and child. Although Gorecki did not claim the link, these songs could be seen as mournful legacies of the horrific genocide carried out by the Nazis in the 1940's. Gorecki himself lost family members during the "Holocaust", and the song in the second movement references words inscribed on the wall of a concentration camp in Poland by a young girl just before her death. Music penetrates directly to the heart of intense suffering, and also fortifies our resolve to prevent cruelty of this magnitude from being witnessed again in history.

Viewing Activity 1: Edvard Munch and Tracey Emin

Perhaps no image has captured the depth of human despair as has the Norwegian artist Edvard Munch's "The Scream" (painted 1893).

Munch: "The Scream". Google Images, widewalls.ch

Munch's early life was blighted by illness and the death of his sister. In contrast to the brilliant sunset gifted by nature in the background, the human figure appears utterly isolated and unable to contain an existential shriek. The painting seems to merge some of our most elemental fears – of loneliness, of loss, of oblivion.

The contemporary British artist, Tracey Emin, finds great resonance in Munch's works. An exhibition at the Royal Academy of Arts in London, titled *"Tracey Emin/Edvard Munch: The Loneliness of the Soul"*, showed from November 15, 2020 to February 28, 2021 and can be accessed at:

https://www.royalacademy.org.uk/exhibition/tracey-emin-edvard-munch

The pathos of Emin's images take on greater poignancy with the looming spectre of Covid and its impact on lives and families, including the death of her cousin.

Viewing activity 2: *Social Dilemma*. Netflix, 2020

"A whole generation is growing up more anxious, fragile and depressed".

Within the last decade, much of our world has been transformed by the astonishing extension of the tentacles of information technology, artificial intelligence, and social media into our daily lives. In some ways, they have created the utopia of connection with others, both near and far, which humans have craved as a bonding species since our genesis. At the same time, they have spawned a cultural crisis which threatens the emotional and political stability of multiple generations and societies. Social psychologist, Jonathan Haidt, points to a gigantic increase in depression and anxiety for American teenagers, beginning around 2010 (which we may now call the inception of the Facebook, Twitter, Instagram, YouTube, Snapchat era); incidents of self-harm went up in girls aged 15-19 by 62%, and for those aged 10-14 by 189%, within the first half of the decade. Suicide rates for 15-19 years old spiked by 70%, and for those 10-14 by 151%, since 1999 (Haidt, in *Social Dilemma*). On the political front, we have noticed the rise of polarization, radicalization, populism, and the collapse of civilized discourse in some of the oldest, largest, and well-established democratic nations. Destructive emotions, including extreme forms of hatred, fear and despair seem to be casting their ominous spell in an era that promised abundance and prosperity never witnessed before in human history.

In the documentary *Social Dilemma*, several inventors and executives of the "tech giants"[29] and social media platforms reflect on the "attention extraction model" that has begun to shape how people think, and even who they are. Each of the companies is competing for our attention, which becomes the "product" that is being sold to the "customers", who are the advertising agencies. Everything that we do online is recorded[30] so that ever more sophisticated algorithms can begin to predict our preferences, whether economic, social, or political, and tailor the advertising and messages to reinforce them. Changes in our behaviour and perceptions, often gradual and imperceptible, arise from the "magical" ability of algorithms to understand something about our minds and influence unconscious habits with the psychology of persuasion. As Tristan Harris points out, this is tapping into our "tribal feeling" of belonging and the importance of gauging whether other people think well of us or not.

However, "we were not evolved to have social approval dosed to us every five minutes" (Harris, in *Social Dilemma*); the constant drama of "likes, hearts, and thumbs up" in social media become conflated with value and "truth", triggering a "fake brittle popularity". Here, the new masters of persuasion are delving deep into the brain stem and our sense of self-worth and identity, which particularly affects young minds and feeds into feelings of insecurity and inadequacy. The vicious cycle nurtures an addiction to the "digital pacifier" when the person is lonely, afraid, or uncertain.

At the civilizational level, too, the exponential advances in technology and artificial intelligence could pose an existential threat. Data scientist

---

[29] Including Facebook, Apple, Google, and Amazon
[30] Harvard Business School professor Shoshana Zukoff calls it "surveillance capitalism", based on unlimited access to data of the general public or consumers.

Cathy O'Neal reminds us that algorithms are not objective; rather they are "opinions embedded in code" and optimized to a definition of "success" that is often driven by the profit motive (O'Neal in *Social Dilemma*). In selling our attention to advertisers, political polarization seems to find fertile ground; "fake news" on Twitter, for example, spreads six times faster than factual reporting, and the system biases toward false information since the truth is considered "boring". A plethora of myths about Covid-19 and the Corona virus circulated on media channels, and Facebook became the medium for hate speech in Myanmar against the minority Rohingya Muslims, culminating in brutal actions and their forcible eviction from the country. Tristan Harris is concerned that social media brings out the worst in society- incivility, alienation, outrage, and lack of trust in each other – sapping the ability to heal itself. Virtual Reality guru, Jaron Lanier, warns that we could "destroy civilization through wilful ignorance" (Lanier in *Social Dilemma*). This coheres well with the Buddhist understanding of destructive and unskilful thought and action, arising from "fundamental ignorance" (Dalai Lama, in Goleman 30).

Transforming the roots of ignorance and suffering into a path of expansion and wellbeing: Buddhist and Neuroscience Perspectives

"All created things are transitory; those who realize this are freed from suffering. This is the path that leads to pure wisdom" (The Buddha, in the *Dhammapada*).

The Buddhist teaching of the Four Noble Truths, affirmed by the Buddha after gaining enlightenment at the age of 35, begins with a statement of startling and determined clarity: "All desire happiness, *sukha*: what is good, pleasant, right, permanent, joyful, harmonious, satisfying, at ease. Yet all find that life brings *dukkha*, just the opposite: frustration, dissatisfaction, incompleteness, suffering, sorrow" (Easwaran 30). The Buddha diagnosed a "pandemic" in the human condition that is universal and pervasive: **life is never entirely satisfying**. The term *dukkha*, from the Pali language of his discourses, connotes "the idea of an ill-fitting cartwheel – bumpy and uncomfortable" (Kulananda 14). It gathers momentum from multiple ruts of daily physical and mental pain, as well as the inability to come to terms with change and the impermanence of objects, relationships, and the mind itself[31]. With his rigorous commitment to inquiry and logic, the Buddha uncovered the source of *dukkha* as an unquenchable yearning and thirst arising from ignorance: "instead of seeing our personality as it really is – an impermanent process - we cling to what we want it to be, something real and separate and permanent. From this ignorance arises '*trishna*'[32], the insistent craving for personal satisfaction" (Easwaran 70). His searing insight reached into all corners of our existence, for the craving includes "not only desire for, and attachment to, sense pleasures, wealth and power, but also desire for and attachment to ideas and ideals, views, opinions, theories, conceptions, and beliefs" (Rahula 30). **In other words, our lives revolve around the mental states that we create for ourselves.**

Unhealthy and unskilful mental states result in a sense of illbeing, trapped in fear and bondage to a destructive and restrictive circle, which mutate into habitual patterns. Poet, Emily Dickinson, memorably called this "the mob within the heart", a crowded, narrowing oppression spiralling into a "**small sense of self**". The Buddha employed another piercing metaphor of the eggshell: "We have no more idea of what life is really like than a chicken has before it hatches. Excitement and depression, fortune and misfortune, pleasure and pain, are storms in a tiny, private, shell-bound realm which we take to be the whole of existence" (Easwaran 47).

---

[31] Born a prince and coddled in luxury, Siddhartha Gautama was forced to confront *dukkha* when he encountered sights of poverty, disease, and death outside the palace, which began the journey away from home and his conditioning toward evolving into the "Buddha" or the "awakened being".

[32] *Trishna,* or thirst, is an appropriate metaphor in a tropical country like India, capturing the intense craving for water on a scorching, dry day.

Contraction lies at the heart of a sense of separateness, of isolation and despair and revulsion of others.

The understanding of the origins of the "small self" becomes the means for its transformation, moving from illbeing to wellbeing. Like any skilled investigator, the Buddha did not promise a quick fix, rather a steady and sustained cultivation of changes in our thought process and a shift in world view. A recognition that reality is much greater than our clinging, confusion, and fear opens the door to an arena that "allows them to be without being lost in them", the foundation of a "spacious, free, liberated, wakeful presence in the world" (Kornfield). Human desire and craving cannot be eliminated, rather remoulded toward the expansion and vitality of the mind. Viewing our internal state of thoughts, emotions, and physical senses as a river, we begin to experience a changing, dynamic current that removes the notion of a fixed or final essence[33]. This altered perspective becomes the bedrock of a creative approach to belief and action: "we are not doomed to simply repeating past patterns of behaviour, endlessly becoming the same old person. **Every moment of life presents an endless array of possibilities**" (Kulananda 60).

The Buddhist vision of inner freedom flowing from an expanded and active mind finds remarkable convergence in contemporary neuroscience. Contrary to the Cartesian view that the human brain is centred in the pineal gland which acts as a "conductor of the self"[34], neuroscience has mapped out highly distributed functions in the brain with no conductor or organizer; rather, the organ is complex, lively and in a state of permanent change (Ricard and Singer). The Buddhist notion of "no self" has been misinterpreted and Gombrich clarifies that the phrase in Sanskrit and Pali translates as "no unchanging self" (Gombrich 9). In fact, the

---

[33] Oxford University Buddhist scholar Richard Gombrich expresses this understanding as "nothing in the world has an unchanging essence" or "there is nothing in our normal experience that never changes" (Gombrich 9).

[34] From the French Enlightenment philosopher Descartes (1596-1650)

"self" is simply "a convenient label for a dynamic stream of experience" (Ricard and Singer); the individual becomes part of a continuum, with no exaggerated sense of self-importance or the grasping ego. The sense of separateness from others is replaced by the chords of connection, well expressed by the great 20th century scientist, Einstein: "A human being… experiences himself, his thoughts and feelings, as something separated from the rest – a kind of optical delusion of his consciousness. This delusion is a kind of prison, restricting us to our personal desires and to affection for a few persons nearest to us. Our task must be to free ourselves from this prison by widening our circle of compassion to embrace all living creatures and the whole of nature in its beauty" (in Easwaran 14).

The practice of mindfulness and kindfulness:

As a physician of the mind, the Buddha followed up his diagnosis of human suffering and its causes with a prescription of effective treatment toward a healthy recovery. He called it the "Eightfold Path", which required sustained practice to refine one's vision, emotion, speech, action, livelihood, effort, awareness, and concentration. He also referred to it as the "Middle Way", with an emphasis upon moderation and balance, a developmental path predicated on the quest for improvement and achieving wellbeing.

Here again, we find a significant confluence of Buddhist perspectives and neuroscience. Richard Davidson, professor of psychiatry and psychology at the University of Wisconsin Madison and head of the Centre for Healthy Minds, credits a meeting with His Holiness the Dalai Lama in 1992 with changing his outlook from a focus on adversity, to a study of positive emotions like kindness and empathy and their impact on the brain. Davidson was aware of the challenges that we identified earlier as sources of illbeing in our times: distractibility, attention deficit, loneliness, negative self-talk impacting self-worth and self-esteem, increase in depression and suicide rates, and a pervasive loss of meaning and purpose in life (Davidson). Now, with our understanding of neuro-plasticity, we could harness the brain's capacity for change and take greater responsibility for training a healthy mind. Davidson identifies four pillars of this transformation:

1. The capacity to focus our attention and resist distraction, including a "meta-awareness" of what our mind is doing, so that we can bring it back to the focal point.

2. Nurturing harmonious inter-personal relationships based on kindness, appreciation and compassion, as well as the larger connections that Einstein urged. As Davidson notes, it doesn't take much to activate this latent tendency in humans.

3. An insight into the narrative that we have about ourselves, in which the negative talk is taken as "reality", replacing that with a healthy narrative that observes the "constellation of thoughts" flowing in the mind.

4. Discovering or pursuing a purpose that points us in a particular direction (Davidson).

In training the mind, we adopt two kinds of learning, which mobilize different brain circuits: the "declarative", which involves learning about things; and the "procedural", which orients the learner towards a process. The adaptability of the brain's wiring was tested in two weeks of compassion training at the University of Wisconsin, involving seven hours of practice. MRI[35] scans of the participants showed changes in the prefrontal cortex (the centre of attention) and strengthening in the ventral striatum, which is crucial for the development of positive emotions. **A healthy mind is a learned behaviour, which endures with practice** (Davidson).

---

[35] Magnetic Resonance Imaging

The "four pillars" identified by Davidson cohere well with the Buddhist practice of **mindfulness**, that culminates in intensive meditative concentration. Buddhist monk, Ajahn Brahm, calls for equal attention to what he calls **kindfulness**, an attitude of respect and affirmation of others. Recognizing the lack of feelings of self-worth and self-esteem as great problems today, which lead to a sense of being never "good enough", Brahm advocates cultivation of the phrase "very good" in our interaction with others, which boosts their confidence and energy. Being mindful of the draining nature of negativity, we can help and inspire others toward a positive outlook. Awareness, compassion for the self and for others brings you "home", a comfortable mental and emotional space.

Learning Activity: SEE - Social, Emotional and Ethical Learning (a curriculum for school students and adults). "The Science of Compassion".
https://compassion.emory.edu

In another instance of collaboration between wisdom traditions and contemporary science, the Centre for Contemplative Science and Compassion-Based Ethics at Emory University in Atlanta, has developed an education programme for the entire age range of school students[36], the culmination of a dialogue with the Dalai Lama since 1998. Social, Emotional and Ethical (SEE) Learning includes 30 age-specific forty minute learning experiences, incorporating a universal, non-sectarian and science-based approach developed by a team of experts in education, developmental psychology, and neuroscience. The Dalai Lama himself urges a universal perspective that goes beyond any particular faith or belief system, "a **secular ethics** that nurtures such basic human values as empathy, tolerance, forgiveness, and love…such values can be cultivated through learning and practice…through the voluntary application of reason and investigation" (SEE foreword). Alongside the traditional

---

[36] The SEE framework is applicable to higher education and professional learning as well.

academic focus on cognitive mastery, "education can, and indeed should be, expanded to foster the values and competencies that lead to greater happiness for both individuals and societies at large" (9). These would include emotional awareness and social skills such as the ability to cooperate and collaborate with others and to deal constructively with conflict.

SEE learning embraces several elements of expansion in the curriculum. There is a sustained focus on fostering the capacity for **attention**, which is seen as foundational to all skills. A more comprehensive anchoring in ethics seeks to create a compassionate, caring attitude that is beneficial, not only to others, but also to oneself for emotional and physical health. The lessons integrate the latest findings in trauma research and trauma-informed care to explore emotions, self-regulation and reflective practices, including the important ability to regulate stress through "body literacy". One of the intended outcomes is to promote **resilience** at individual, interpersonal, social and cultural levels. The holistic view promotes increased awareness of our inter-dependence and possible contributions to systems as responsible global citizens (11). These features play a prominent role in structuring the SEE framework, the three dimensions of awareness, compassion[37] and engagement manifested in three domains: the personal, social, and systems.

In keeping with its investigative outlook, the SEE learning includes **critical thinking** as one of its primary "learning threads", inviting exploration of topics through logical reasoning, multiple perspectives, dialogue and debate. Students are thus encouraged to develop a deeper personal understanding and to "embrace their questions" (21). This thread also nurtures epistemic humility, a recognition that our views are partial, limited and open to change. Scientific perspectives, drawn from biology,

---

[37] Dr. Thupten Jinpa, developer of Stanford University's Compassion Cultivation Training program, explains compassion as "a sense of concern that arises when we are confronted by another person's suffering and feel motivated to see that suffering relieved…(it) connects the feeling of empathy to acts of kindness, generosity, and other expressions of our altruistic tendencies" (SEE 15).

psychology, and neuroscience, highlight empirical observation and the study of cause and effect in understanding emotions and their impact on personal and communal wellbeing. Engaged learning channels students into active, participatory strategies of cooperative planning, creative expression, service to others, and an ecological outlook. The thread of **reflective practices** deepens attention toward the individual's inner experience and the internalization of skills which support focus building experiences (24).

A pedagogical model that combines scientific inquiry, cultivation of ethical values, awareness and enhanced attention, active participation, and reflective evaluation could go a long way in confronting the distractibility, negative personal narratives, isolation, hostility and other roots of emotional suffering and unskilful states of mind in our times. The pace remains moderate, too, since the goals of SEE are not seen as benchmarks, but rather as a "direction of learning" on the journey to developing enduring capabilities in emotion and cognition (25). The framework sets up a foundation for the growth mindset.

The Growth Mindset: A Mental Map for navigating emotions and life

"I don't divide the world into the weak and the strong or the successes and the failures. *I divide the world into the learners and non-learners*".

Benjamin Barber, sociologist[38]

Stanford University psychologist Carol Dweck, basing her research on the learning approaches and actions of her students, coined the terms "fixed mindset" and "growth mindset" to highlight two contrasting

---

[38] Quoted in Dweck (16).

attitudes that shape our mental world or "mind maps". As she points out, **entering a mindset is entering a world that drives every aspect of our lives**, as children and adults, impacting schooling, work, creativity, sports, relationships and parenting. "In one world – the world of fixed traits – success is about proving you're smart or talented. Validating yourself. In the other – the world of changing qualities – it's about stretching yourself to learn something new. Developing yourself" (Dweck 15). In the fixed mindset, failure is seen as a setback, a judgement on your abilities and talents. In the growth mindset, failure is viewed as an avenue for improvement, moving toward fulfilling your potential. The two phrases that embody the growth mindset are *"not yet"* and *"learn from failure"*, a blueprint for effort, determination and grit.

As a psychologist and educator, Dweck was interested in investigating mental depression, which threatens to become a scourge in our societies. Measuring students' mindsets and examining diary entries in college campuses, she discovered that those with fixed mindsets had higher levels of depression. The analyses showed that "this was because they ruminated over their problems and setbacks…tormenting themselves with the idea that the setbacks meant they were incompetent or unworthy"; the failures had basically labelled them (38). It also left them without the will to take actions to solve their problems, a spiralling effect that is often observed in depression. In comparison, "the *more* depressed people with the growth mindset felt, the *more* they took actions to confront their problems, the *more* they made sure to keep up with their schoolwork, the *more* they kept up with their lives. The worse they felt, the more determined they became!" (38). These attributes can translate into some ironic consequences: "The top is where the fixed mindset people hunger to be, but it's where many growth minded people arrive as a by-product of their enthusiasm for what they do" (48). Mindsets could also determine our outlook on some of society's stinging arrows such as stereotypes and bias. Those with a fixed mindset may internalize them as permanent qualities whereas "a growth mindset helps people to see prejudice for what it is – *someone else's* view of them – and to confront it with their confidence and abilities intact" (78).

Neuroscience supports the positive impact of the growth mindset in the brain. As Professor Andrew Huberman explains, there is an attachment of reward systems in the brain to the pursuit of a goal. The neuro-modulator[39] dopamine is released in the effort and 'friction' process, so that "**the effort is the path**" (Huberman). Whereas dopamine is a "feel good" factor for an external activity, serotonin and oxytocin heighten the "reward circuits" in actions that result in internal states of content-ment. In fact, Huberman argues for viewing the growth mindset as a **verb**, since our brains are "wired for the puzzle rather than the outcome" (Huberman). In engaging with and enhancing the plasticity of the brain, we begin to internalize the neural circuits to achieve our objectives with virtually no limits. Huberman approvingly cites one of the golfing greats, Tiger Woods: *"I just trust the process"*. Even with supreme athletes like Woods, there is no fixed benchmark of perfection; there is always room to move their skill another notch while providing incredible joy to specta-tors and lovers of the game. Jack Kornfield makes the case for the growth mindset with precision: "***to be enlightened is to be without anxiety about non-perfection***" (Kornfield).

Viewing activity: Growth Mindset Starts Early
What Growth Mindset Means for Kids
https://www.youtube.com/watch?v=66yaYmUNOx4
March 25, 2019. Accessed 11.3.2021

Third grade student, Rebecca Chang, from Shekou International School explains how she challenged herself to run for the Student Council at the age of nine. She displays public speaking skills at a tender age which

---

39 Neuromodulators like dopamine, serotonin, and oxytocin "enhance the activity of particular brain circuits and brain areas and suppress the activity of others" (Huberman).

would be the envy of most adults! Environments that stimulate the growth mindset, both at home and school, assist in nurturing lifelong habits that inspire effort, resilience, and the joy of discovering new skills and abilities. They become natural allies of the brain's plasticity and its reward circuits.

Learning Activities: *The Growth Mindset Coach* (Ulysses Press, Berkeley), 2016.

Authors Annie Brock and Heather Hundley offer a teacher's month-by-month handbook to encourage the development of the growth mindset with a series of activities and self-assessment exercises for school students. Parents and adults would also benefit from the practical applications contained here; among the memorable chapter titles are "My Brain is like a Muscle that grows!"; "Mistakes are opportunities for learning"; and "There's a difference between not knowing and not knowing yet!".

The Happiness Gene: How Cultures Nurture Joy and Wellbeing

After having overcome the obstacles of nature and the elements in their quest for survival as a species, humans turned their attention to probing the sources of satisfaction and flourishing that flowed from relative abundance and the luxury of leisure time. Over the centuries, our societies and civilizations gifted us an incredible array of beliefs and rituals that we can imbibe in our journey toward physical and mental wellbeing. We could call this generous legacy the "happiness gene", ours to nurture and blossom.

Our earliest societies recognized the need for individuals to discover their own strengths and sources of personal flowering. The Australian aboriginal practice of "walkabout" involved adolescent male initiates in rites of passage that deepened their connection to the land. They followed ancient 'songlines' to find food and shelter from the rocks and trees; "in this quest they would develop the deep self-awareness that only comes from solitude" (Happy 25). Similarly, in the First Nations of Canada and the USA, the "vision quest" involved a period of fasting and isolation during which "the quester meditates deeply, calling on spirit guides to reveal to them the necessary direction of their lives" (47). In these practices, we find the genesis of today's "growth mindset", the ability to confront challenges and move toward the realization of goals and personal purpose. They also encourage us to transcend the "small self" of everyday anxieties, worries, and discomforts in the direction of the expanded "big self", creating the space for creativity and ingenuity.

Groups and social bonding bestow further springs of pleasure. The Danish "*hygge*"[40] induces "a sense of cosiness and inner warmth" (111) – like sharing a nice bottle of wine and engaging in conversation with friends and family around a fire. The presence of the domestic cat or dog adds to the sense of pure comfort and contentment.

The German *Stamtisch* or "regulars' table" helps to link people beyond family to those with common passions and hobbies, ranging from "professions to politics to languages to parenthood, giving participants the chance to discuss their experiences, network and express whatever is on their minds"[41] (85). To partake in a communal endorphin release, head to the Shanghai Bund in China – one of the most enchanting sights for me was to be greeted at dawn with groups of old and young alike stretching and swaying gracefully in the motions of Tai Chi, repeating and preserving the flowing rhythms of their ancestors. When the community connects with a force greater than itself, the springs of gratification run deep. In Israel, the Jewish festival of *Tu BiShvat* is celebrated with the planting of trees in the month of *Shevat* (January/February), accompanied

---

[40] The closest in English pronunciation may be "whoo-ger".

[41] The internet, of course, opens up multiple possibilities of (virtual) *Staamtisch*.

by children singing songs about the almond tree and eating dates, walnuts and apricots (31). Planting seeds in the dead of winter reminds us of the resilience and eternal renewal cycles of nature and the need to honour its deliberate tempo of growth, with implications for human development and thriving[42].

Indeed, humans have celebrated and worshipped nature from an early stage of our existence, moving from fearing it as a threat to perceiving it as a reliable ally. Enjoying the fruits of its abundance is now encoded in our cultural genes, with Thanksgiving festivals abounding in all corners of the world. The Ethiopian Buna (Coffee) ceremony is presided over by a woman in a traditional white dress, the heady scent of incense matched by the intoxicating aroma of freshly roasted and brewed coffee, which is gracefully poured from a long-spouted *jebena* (59). The guests must imbibe three cups, with the third or *baraka* invoking a blessing. Echoes of this gratitude can be heard today from countless homes and Starbucks outlets as the dark animating liquid courses through expectant veins. The "cup that cheers" also finds its aesthetic finesse in the Japanese tea ceremony; stylized reverence for a beverage that generates intense relaxation, calmness and agreeable companionship. The sweet partner to our caffeine pleasures gets its own recognition in the Crop Over festival in Barbados and other islands in the Caribbean. From the 1780's, plantation workers celebrated the end of the sugar-cane harvest with a procession of carts laden with the fruits of their labour. Today, their descendants make merry to the rousing beats of calypso music, an occasion for parades and partying culminating in the Grand Kadooment, "a spectacular procession of costumed revellers dancing through the streets"[43] (109).

---

[42] Similarly, the Chinese celebrate their New Year as the "Spring Festival" in January/February, when the earth seems frozen and incapable of fertility.

[43] Comparable thrilling spectacles would be the Carnival in Brazil, Mardi Gras in New Orleans (USA) and the Holi festival of splashing color in India to welcome the advent of Spring.

Community ties generate togetherness and inclusion, rescuing us from the risks of isolation and despondency. In the Pacific Tokelau and Cook Islands, the custom of *inati* (sharing) ensures that the daily catch from the sea is distributed equitably by the village council (119). Humble fishermen and subsistence farmers in Chile offer their toil to each other in *minga*, echoed in the practice and ethic of *gotong royong* (mutual assistance and cooperation) in Indonesia. Elevated into a principle of interdependent welfare in several African societies, *ubuntu* could be translated as "I am only a person through other people" (125). Children benefit from its warm and joyful ambience, a recognition that "it takes a village to raise a child". A five-day Ubuntu Festival every July in Cape Town, South Africa, nudges the value of human connections further. The Italians do not need a special day to foster good neighbourly relationships; the daily *passeggiata* brings people of all ages for an evening stroll through the pavements and squares in villages, towns and cities to share conversation, drink and ingest *gelato*[44] at a relaxed pace. No wonder the Italians initiated the Slow Living movement! The Himalayan kingdom of Bhutan elevates happiness to a national goal, as King Wangchuk exhorted his citizens to opt for "Gross National Happiness" rather than the usual material and consumerist indicators of wealth. The blending of Buddhist ethics and spectacular mountain landscapes contribute to Bhutan's air of contentment, civility and equanimity.

As we have discovered earlier in this chapter, the acceptance and embracing of change opens the door to emotional health and fulfilment. Not surprisingly, Buddhist societies include practices that rejoice in transient feelings and beliefs. In Thailand's incandescent *Loy Krathong*, held every November, candle-fuelled paper lanterns rise up into the night sky, symbolically carrying away the burdens of anxiety and worries that may have accumulated in our lives. Tibetan sand paintings of intricate *mandalas*,

---

[44] The distinctively Italian ice cream.

crafted with loving care and skilled artistry over several days or weeks, are swept away after completion, a reminder of the inevitable footprints of time. "Half of the sand is distributed among the audience, to disperse its healing through the room; the other half is fed to the nearest river, to carry its healing throughout the world" (23). The Jains, a group in India reared in non-violence and benevolence, recognize the perils of clinging onto anger and hostility toward others. At the *Paryushan Parva*, held annually, days of prayer and meditation are followed by a ceremonial asking for a granting of forgiveness. To forgive others flows from recognizing our own imperfections and forgiving the self. Getting rid of mental and physical clutter becomes a powerful source of renewal. At the time of the *Chun Jie*, Chinese New Year, families scrub their homes in a thorough spring cleaning, an impetus to "sweep away that junk at home, at work, in your relationships, in your mind"[45] (49). The greatest challenge of change for most humans is coming to terms with one's mortality. The *Dia de Muertos* (Day of Death) in Mexico, held every November, confronts this reality with a colourful and undaunted celebration of life. The dead are welcomed back as grinning life-sized papier-mache skeletons, offered food, flowers and candles, and accompanied by mariachi bands and dancing. Death is converted into a fiesta!

Now that we are aware of the adaptable, flexible, live-wired nature of our brain, learning at all ages becomes a biological imperative. The Balinese pay homage to the goddess of knowledge, *Saraswati*, with offerings of flowers and incense to books and musical instruments on the last day of their *Pawukon* calendar[46]. This reverence for wisdom resonates in

---

[45] Japanese author, Marie Kondo, explores the art of de-cluttering in several popular books, including "*The Life Changing Magic of Tidying Up*" and in the Netflix series "*Tidying up with Marie Kondo*".

[46] The Balinese year comprises 210 days, six months of 35 days each. Annual celebrations and festivals thus recur on this enchanting island more frequently than elsewhere!

the heavens as the aromatic incense wafts upward. Learning is the most reliable composer of our happiness and joy.

Listening Experience 1: *The Happiness Lab* with Dr. Laurie Santos, Yale University (podcast).

The course taught by Dr. Santos at Yale, "Psychology and the Good Life", became the most popular among its students. She has distilled much of its wisdom in the episodes of the podcast, which range from lessons absorbed from the "ancients" to sources of comfort and cheer in our times, including a segment on the challenges of the coronavirus. As a "lab", the episodes carry a soothing fusion of experimental practicality and optimism, striking a chord in all ages.

Listening Experience 2: Antonin Dvorak: Symphony no. 9, "From the New World"

Gimnazija Kranj Symphony Orchestra, Nejc Bejan (conductor)
https://www.youtube.com/watch?v=O_tPb4JFgmw
December 26, 2018. Accessed: 16.3.2021

Music expresses the entire gamut of human emotions. Earlier, we heard the tones of intense sorrow and suffering in Gorecki's third symphony. Now, we can turn to sounds of elation and exuberance that light up the pleasure centres in a glow of delight and fulfilment.

The Bohemian (Czech) composer Dvorak wrote this masterpiece in 1893 while on an extended stay in America. In the earlier movements, there are hints of nostalgia and homesickness as Dvorak used melodies from his homeland. However, these are transformed by the inventive spirit and optimism that he imbibed in the "New World", the finale, a rousing celebration of creative passion. Fittingly, Neil Armstrong left behind a recording of this symphony after the first human steps on the moon, a sparkling cosmic gift. This performance by the Slovakian orchestra conveys the intensity and enchantment of the music with youthful zest, a thrilling auditory and emotional experience that would please the heavens.

Listening Experience 3: Franz Joseph Haydn: Cello Concertos

Mstislav Rostropovich, Academy of St. Martin in the Fields (director Iona Brown)
https://www.youtube.com/watch?v=IVIqiR2z0ew
November 11, 2017 (recorded 1975). Accessed: 2.3.2021

No other Western composer seems to compare with Franz Haydn (1732-1809) in the "happiness quotient": his music always fills me with inexplicable exultation. The two cello concertos, with the Russian maestro "Slava" as the soloist, are amongst the most beautiful and joyous expressions of the human spirit. They give me the sense of "coming home" to a deep inner chord of serene satisfaction.

Sources/Citations

Brock, Annie and Hundley, Heather. 2016. *The Growth Mindset Coach*. Berkeley, Ulysses Press.

Davidson, Richard J. *How Mindfulness Changes the Emotional Life of our Brains*. Ted X, San Francisco.
https://www.youtube.com/watch?v=7CBfCW67xT8
December 13, 2019. Accessed: 14.3.2021.

Dweck, Carol S. 2006. *Mindset: The New Psychology of Success*. New York, Random House.

Easwaran, Eknath. 1986. *The Dhammapada*. London, Arkada (Penguin).

Goleman, Daniel, ed. 1997. *Healing Emotions*. Boston, Shambhala.

Gombrich, Richard. 2009. *What the Buddha Thought*. London, Equinox.

Hansard, Christopher. 2003. *The Tibetan Art of Positive Thinking.* London, Hodder and Stoughton.

Happy: The Secrets to Happiness from the Cultures of the World. 2011. Melbourne, Lonely Planet.

Huberman, Andrew. *Unleash Your Brain Power and Growth Mindset.* https://www.youtube.com/watch?v=t7QBZOH0BFU August 11, 2020. Accessed: 7.9.2020

Kornfield, Jack. *Joy and its Causes.* www.youtube.com/watch?v=oZs5RXm__IQ&t=2307s April 12, 2017. Accessed: 17.8.2020

Kulananda. 1996. *Principles of Buddhism.* London, Harper Collins.

MacFarquhar, Larissa. "*The Mind-Expanding Ideas of Andy Clark*". The New Yorker, April 2, 2018.

Rahula, Walpola. 1967. *What the Buddha Taught.* Bedford, Gordon Fraser.

Ricard, Matthieu and Wolf Singer. *Buddhism Meets Neuroscience.* www.youtube.com/watch?v=Nne3BJ-p7Yg&t=2113s February 7, 2018. Accessed: 2.3.2021

Richards, G. 2005. '*Emotions into Words – or Words into Emotions?*', in Harding, Jennifer and E. Deidre Pribram, eds. 2009. *Emotions: A Cultural Studies Reader.* London, Routledge.

SEE. 2019. *Social, Emotional, Ethical Learning.* Emory University, Atlanta. Centre for Contemplative Science and Compassion-Based Ethics. https://compassion.emory.edu

Singh, Harishchandra Lal. 2000. *Essence of Buddhism.* New Delhi, Adarsh.

The Fifth Circle of Joy

The understanding and mastery of emotions at the fourth circle becomes the catalyst for an explosive creativity at the fifth, centred at the larynx. The "voice box" awarded us a primary distinguishing biological bounty, and we have repaid that with an incredible celebration of our expressive faculty. The scale of human inventiveness is truly staggering, feeding generously from the feast of an emotional synthesis. We encounter here an accelerated animation; numerous avenues of playful exploration.

True to its distinctive feature, this circle privileges the faculty of speech and its complementary extensions in song, drama and the written word. Age, culture, and social status pose few barriers to creative outpouring, especially in our era of dynamic change and striving for inclusive perspectives. We begin to hear stories of historical discrimination, suffering, conflict, disruption and exclusion. The emergence of these voices creates the space for reckoning with, and honouring, myriad experiences, to avoid what Nigerian author Chimamanda Adichie calls "the danger of a single story". The very act of expression begins the path of healing, opening the doors to multiple moments of joy as we savour the enveloping magic of each tone, of every note and sound.

Our biological inheritance also coupled speech with hearing; in fact, the ratio of one mouth and two ears indicates a clear signal of the relative significance of each! This circle, thus, continues to privilege the vitality of **listening** as a durable skill. Here, it also blends into exquisite pleasure as we luxuriate in the sounds of elegant poetry, the dramatic cadences of theatre and debate, and the lyrical rapture of music. While basking in the glory of creative treasures imbibed from artistic traditions far and near, we are also reminded that creativity remains a universal bequest, open to zestful nurturance in each individual. Here the motif of the "**mental map**" takes on added significance, now informed by the ability to forge new directions in the emergence of a unique worldview. Whether collective or personal, creativity sparks catharsis.

This circle further honours **diversity** and **plurality** as the foundational seeds of creative joy. Here again, we draw generously upon Braudel's "second cycle" of civilizational learning, looking at the extraordinary range of human conception in making our lives and our living spaces more agreeable and enchanting. Often, this achievement has been accompanied by an ennobling humility, as we recognize the sustaining power of higher forces in gratitude and worship. Braudel's "third cycle" is not confined to the natural environment, but carries implications as well for the **ecology of the mind.** Just as the garbage pickers of Cateura in Paraguay convert trash into music, we are invited to remove the dross or, as the brilliant 19th century Indian thinker, Swami Vivekananda, put it, to "cast out the cobwebs" in our minds. The cleansing and expansion of the mind gathers gravity and pulsation as Tibetan choirs transport us along the utterly beguiling sounds of multi-phonic chanting. We move closer to the centers of cosmic energy.

The womb of creative flair

Stanford University neuroscientist David Eagleman calls creativity our "biological mandate". The gift of a larger prefrontal cortex in the human brain makes us the "runaway species", generating possibilities at a blazing pace and filtering them to spark novel combinations with the capacity to move others. This "live wired" organ continually reconfigures itself in a passionate coupling with the outside world, well beyond the confines of its cave-like skull (Eagleman). The eager exploration begins early in the uninhibited, adventurous realm of childhood.

Poems by four-year-old Wang Jing Xing[47]

2019.5.3 独语诗：自由

自由就是孤单，

是妈妈，公主，王子都不在，

只有一个人。

自由又是快乐，

自己的事情自己做。

自由本来就是

孤单和快乐在一起。

——笔录自寻寻三岁零七个月看《冰雪奇缘》漫画时的独语

Freedom

Freedom is like solitude,

All thoughts of Mama, Princess and Prince are away,

Only oneself.

Freedom is also Joy,

One's own thoughts, own deeds.

Freedom is just so,

Solitude and Joy combined.

---

[47] Transcribed by his father, Wang Xuebin, my former colleague at Keystone Academy, Beijing. English translation: Mr. Luke Hughes, consultant at Keystone Academy.

2019.5.13 对话诗：太阳妈妈

太阳妈妈落山后就回家了。

她要去照顾她的八个宝宝。

她会和每个宝宝说我爱你，

给每个宝宝巧克力、棒棒糖和冰激凌。

但她最爱地球宝宝，

她亲遍了地球宝宝，

然后地球宝宝就有了人类。

——笔录自寻寻三岁零六个多月时与寻爸的对话

Mother Sun

Mother Sun has returned from hiding behind the hill.

She wants to nourish her eight Little Ones.

She says to each of them 'I love You',

To each she gives chocolate, lollipops and ice creams.

But the one she loves best is Little Earth.

She kisses Little Earth,

Then Little Earth bears Little People.

2019.5.21 寻寻诗 美与爱

人在地上生活，

鱼在水里生活。

美的人爱美的人，

美的鱼爱美的鱼。

美的人也可以爱美的鱼。

因为爱就是美呀！

Beautiful and Love

Human lives on ground,

Fish lives in water.

Beautiful people love beautiful people.

Beautiful fish love beautiful fish.

Beautiful people also can love beautiful fish.

Because actually,

love is beautiful.

2019.4.11 独语诗: 路灯

路灯像鱼篮, 灯像发光的鱼。

发光, 发光, 照亮树, 照亮黑色的河。

让我一直玩, 像鱼一样。

————笔录自寻寻三岁六个多月时在操场上的独语

Street lamps

Street lamps like fish baskets,

Their lights like luminous fish.

Glistening, glistening,

Lighting up the trees, lighting up the dark, black river.

Oh, let me always be playing, just like those fish.

Jing Xing is heir to a glorious tradition of aesthetic nurturing in five thousand years of Chinese civilization. As Dr. Eagleman points out, creativity builds upon a constant tweaking of the past, a combination of novelty and familiarity using "bending, breaking, and blending" (Eagleman). The four-year old uses familiar objects and emotions – he bends each one with a theme, breaks them into separate components, and blends them with similes and metaphors. These are astounding insights from a four year old mind, a merging of the cognitive and the emotional. The "preschool" brain is fresh, inventive, plastic, raring for further stimulation in a supportive milieu[48]. A rapturous discovery for me was Pak Udjo's Angklung School in Bandung, Indonesia. Here, an orchestra of youngsters ranging from ages 2 to 15 entertain the audience with thrilling tunes on the *"angklung"*, a bamboo instrument, accompanied by flutes and drums. To witness two and three year old girls and boys perform with focused attention and aplomb (with the occasional wandering away from the stage!) is incredibly heart-warming. One could feel the gentle and caring guidance of the old master, Pak Udjo (now succeeded by his son), instilling in his young charges, confidence and the joy of rhythmic precision. After the show, the performers involve the audience in learning the basics of the instrument, an inclusive embrace of merry melody. It was one of the happiest experiences of my life.

Listening Experience: Saung Angklung Udjo Plays Mozart's Symphony no. 40

https://www.youtube.com/watch?v=Mh2S6L78IVc
December 28, 2013. Accessed: 24.3.2021

In a wonderful tribute from one culture to another, the Udjo Angklung orchestra plays extracts from the first movement of the beloved 40th. symphony by the immortal composer Wolfgang Mozart. Enjoy the "goose bumps" from this enthralling musical blending!

---

[48] Sadly, most schooling stifles creativity in the search for "standardization" and "the right answer".

Creative exuberance: narrative plenitude and myriad voices

Those who tell the stories rule the world.
Hopi Native American proverb

As with objects, stories take on a power and significance of their own. We are a story-telling species, an atavistic link to tales recounted by our forebears around camp fires; they are not just a biological mandate, but have evolved into social and cultural mandates as well. As stories mingle with history, they magnify the ability of rulers to shape the narratives in their own likeness, sculpting an imagination of superiority of a particular perspective and the exclusion of others. The Nigerian author Chimamanda Ngozi Adichie calls this "**the danger of a single story**" (Adichie). In the context of the colonization of large parts of Africa, Asia, and the Americas by European nations from the 16th. to 20th centuries, the "single story" privileged European cultural notions and degraded the colonized. Chimamanda refers to depictions of Africans as "beasts", "half-devil and half-child", and native groups in the Americas and Australasia were similarly tarred with the brush of "savagery" and "infantilism" to justify their subjugation[49]. Stories were a powerful ingredient in the "colonization of the mind", seeping into the minds of impressionable and vulnerable children (Adichie). We are now living in a period where the suppressed voices of the colonized have entered the global discourse, articulating their own narratives and worldviews. An explosion of emotion, imagination and lived experience has moved us into a many splendored realm of literary richness.

On the African continent, writers like Chinua Achebe sparked the mental shift towards a more balanced representation, a legacy inherited by

---

[49] Nigerian poet, Niyi Osundare, notes that "Africa's truth has always been at the mercy of the fiction of others" (in Patke 11).

women writers, Chimamanda and Yaa Gyasi, from Ghana. Their stories encompass the entire spectrum of human personality and the ambiguities of human existence, formed often in the context of a haunting past. Chimamanda's *"Half of a Yellow Sun"* builds upon the experiences of her own family in the Nigerian Civil War from 1967 to 1970, when the Igbo ethnic group attempted to secede by forming the Republic of Biafra. As an Igbo, she had to confront the trauma of the death of her grandfathers and images of malnourished children, but the novel is a celebration of the resilience and dignity of her people as well. As she observes, stories may "dispossess and malign, but they (can) also empower and humanize" (Adichie). The character that resonated most with her was Ugwu, the houseboy; like her, "he is eager to learn, asks questions, and dreams" (*Half Of*). Social class may no longer be a hindrance to advancement in the rapidly developing nations of Africa, Asia, Central and South America.

In her novel *"Homegoing"*, Yaa Gyasi tackles the most vexed legacy of the African past, arising from the trans-Atlantic slave trade with the Americas[50]. Centred at the Cape Coast Castle in Ghana, the story of two half-sisters, Effia and Esi, traces the parallel lives of seven generations over three centuries in Ghana and America. Effia marries the British governor, living a privileged life at the castle, while Esi is enslaved in the dungeon below, a striking proximity of free Ghanaian women walking above their captive sisters below. The complicity of African chiefdoms and rival groups in the slave trade adds a complex layer to the profit motive of European colonizers, but nothing can conceal the monstrous conditions in the dungeon and during the "middle passage" ship voyage to the New World. Caribbean poet, Derek Walcott, captures the

---

[50] A poignant reminder of fraught racial relations erupted in May 2020 after the murder of African-American George Floyd at the hands of the police in the city of Minneapolis, triggering a "Black Lives Matter" movement in several parts of the world.

difficulties and the necessity of keeping that experience in collective memory (from *Laventille*, in Patke 85):

> *The middle passage never guessed its end.*
> *This is the height of poverty*
> *for the desperate and the black;*
> *climbing, we could look back*
> *with widening memory*
> *on the hot, corrugated-iron sea*
> *whose horrors we all*
> *shared.*

Gyasi brings this remembrance, the voice of the slaves, into our midst. These are stories of remarkable resilience amidst degradation and exploitation, the ability to create a culture with adoptive families and an adopted but transformed faith. She is able to immerse her characters in the "fabulist" mode of West African folklore and fable, in which "home-going" implies that the soul or spirit of the slave goes back home after death. The "middle passage" is reversed, for "you carry home with you, wherever you go" (Gyasi).

Similarly, Vietnamese refugees who fled to America at the end of the Vietnam War in the 1970's have begun to recreate "home" in their new setting. Author Viet Thanh Nguyen grew up in "Little Saigon" in Orange County, California, which he calls a "work of collective memory" (Viet). Food plays an important part in the reaffirmation of identity, as the American palate begins to delight in "pho" and other Vietnamese delicacies. However, for Nguyen, the more urgent task is to generate narratives that counter the stereotypical and dehumanizing portrayals of Vietnamese in American popular culture, such as the film *"Apocalypse Now"*. With novels like *"The Sympathizer"* and *"The Committed"*, he attempts to depict the full range of human possibility in his characters, so that Vietnamese and other Asian Americans may reclaim "the luxury of mediocrity" (Viet) that is accorded the majority culture in its literary space.

No group in America has endured stereotypical portrayal, decimation and marginalization to the extent of the Native American. This pattern was repeated in the treatment of indigenous people in Australia, Africa, Central and South America, and parts of Asia in the period of European conquest and colonization. Their voices were stifled for centuries, but not stilled. Native Nations poetry has begun to reclaim the emotional and cultural arena of a richly diverse storytelling tradition, with important lessons for our frenzied, dislocated, mechanical modes of living. Gail Tremblay from the Onondaga and Mi'Kmaq nations expresses the ability of her people to inhabit different worlds of time and seasonality, preserving a link to the expansive rhythms of nature and art.

Indian Singing in 20th Century America[51]

We wake; we wake the day,
the light rising in us like sun-
our breath a prayer brushing
against the feathers in our hands.
We stumble out into streets;
patterns of wires invented by strangers
are strung between eye and sky,
and we dance in two worlds,
inevitable as seasons in one,
exotic curiosities in the other
which rushes headlong down highways,
watches us from car windows, explains

---

[51] The mis-naming of native people in the Americas as "Indians" was the first step in the attempt by European colonizers to annihilate their existing civilizations and identities. Gail Tremblay uses "Indian" here to emphasize the continuity of discrimination against Native nations.

us to its children in words
that no one could ever make
sense of. The image obscures
the vision, and we wonder
whether anyone will ever hear
our own names for the things
we do. Light dances in the body,
surrounds all living things –
even the stones sing
although their songs are infinitely
slower than the ones we learn
from trees. No human voice lasts
long enough to make such music sound.
Earth breath eddies between factories
and office buildings, caresses the surface
of our skin; we go to jobs, the boss
always watching the clock to see
that we're on time. He tries to shut
our magic and hopes we'll make
mistakes or disappear. We work
fast and steady and remember
each breath alters the composition
of the air. Change moves relentless,
the pattern unfolding despite their planning –
we're always there- singing round dance
songs, remembering what supports
our life – impossible to ignore.

Gail Tremblay (in Harjo 42-43).

Mary Tallmountain of the Koyukon nation expresses the timeless wisdom of her elder and the pathos of a universal emotion.

There is no word for Goodbye

Sokoya, I said, looking through
the net of wrinkles into
wise black pools
of her eyes.

What do you say in Athabascan
when you leave each other?
What is the word
for goodbye?

A shade of feeling rippled
the wind-tanned skin.
Ah, nothing, she said,
watching the river flash.

She looked at me close.
We just say, Tlaa. That means,
See you.
We never leave each other.
When does your mouth
say goodbye to your heart?

She touched me light
as a bluebell.
You forget when you leave us;
you're so small then.
We don't use that word.
We always think you're coming back,
but if you don't,

we'll see you someplace else.
You understand.
There is no word for goodbye.

Mary Tallmountain (in Harjo 188-189)

Universality of emotions gush from the story-telling genius of the Central and South American continents as well. In her captivating novel *"A Long Petal of the Sea"*, Chilean author Isabel Allende presents the beauty of love as something that transcends an "outburst of hormones". Love happens in many ways, and the love of Victor and Roser happens "in reverse", moving from convenience to deep friendship to a passionate affair. This is a mature bonding, mirroring Isabel's own passion at age 77: "all stories are love stories…and the greatest are told by time" (*A Long Petal…*). This love was "a luminous discovery…she fell in love with a tall, tough stranger, his features sculpted like dark wood, his eyes gentle and his clothes freshly ironed, someone who was capable of surprising her and making her laugh with silly remarks, who gave her pleasure as if he had memorized the map of her body, who cradled her all night long so that she fell asleep and woke nestled against his shoulder…In her fifties, Roser was revealed to him as sensual, filled with enthusiasm, with an endless reserve of fearless energy…He never imagined that at his age he could fall in love like an adolescent or feel desire like wildfire. He looked at her enraptured, because still intact beneath her appearance as a mature woman was the innocent, formidable little girl Roser must have been when she looked after goats on a hillside in Catalonia" (Allende 252-53).

Time and history also shape a story of displacement, of fortitude and resilience, with deep resonance in the multiple refugee and migrant crises in our midst today. Victor and Roser are displaced twice, from Spain to Chile at the end of the Spanish Civil War in 1939, and from Chile to Venezuela after the military coup in 1973. Luckily, they are well received in both host countries and make stellar contributions to their adopted homes: "Venezuela received Victor with the same easy going generosity with which it took in thousands of immigrants from many parts of the world…(it) was one of the few democracies left in a continent dominated by heartless regimes and thuggish military juntas…There were so many natural resources that nobody killed themselves working; there was plenty of space and opportunity for whoever wanted to come and set themselves up. Life was one long party, with a great sense of freedom and a profound sense of equality. Any excuse was good enough to celebrate with music, dancing, and alcohol" (253-54). Fifty years later, history has dealt an ironic and cruel blow to Venezuela, now reduced to an impoverished state under a repressive dictatorship and with millions of its citizens fleeing to other countries.

Time does not spare anyone. Roser's death from cancer leaves Victor with the prospect of solitude and lonely aging, but he continues to serve others as an experienced surgeon and to forestall his son's advice for remarriage: "The possibility of getting married again sent a shiver down his spine; he was happy with the company of his animals. It wasn't true that he talked to himself; he was talking to the dogs, the parrot, and the cat…He would arrive home at night to tell his pets all that had happened during the day. They were his audience on the rare occasions he became sentimental, and listened to him as he closed his eyes and named objects in the house or the flora and fauna in the garden. That was his way of focusing his memory and his attention, the way other old people did crossword puzzles" (290). The vulnerability of aging does not preclude steely determination, as Victor finds reasons to defend his position as a widower: "the freedom to talk to himself, to curse and complain without witnesses about the private discomforts he would never admit to in public. Pride. That was what his wife and son had often accused him of, but his determination to appear hale and hearty to everyone else was not pride but vanity, a trick to defend himself against decrepitude. As well as walking erect and disguising his tiredness, he also tried to avoid other symptoms of old age: meanness, mistrust, ill temper, resentment, and bad habits such as no longer shaving every day, repeating the same stories over and over, talking about himself, his ailments, or money" (296). After meeting his long lost daughter from another relationship, "it seemed to Victor he was listening to Roser in her final moments, reminding him that we human beings are gregarious, we're not programmed for solitude, but to give and receive" (313).

The cycles of time in Allende, grounded in history and real events, reach toward wider levels of human consciousness and revelation. She is heir to the genre of "magical realism" that burst on the literary scene with the works of Colombian author, Gabriel Garcia Marquez. In "*One Hundred Years of Solitude*", "*The Autumn of the Patriarch*", "*Love in the time of Cholera*", Marquez used the rich tradition of oral story telling inherited from his grandmother to create a world in which village fables and superstition are considered real and the realm of technology and science appear unreal or surreal. Just as Allende reverses the course of love, Marquez reverses the expectations of the modern world. Salman Rushdie, who was deeply influenced by Marquez in his own stories of "magical realism" from the Indian subcontinent[52], observes that it, in fact, has "deep roots in the real, and illuminates it in beautiful, unexpected ways...imagination is used to enrich reality, not to escape from it...if it was only magic, it wouldn't matter and would be just whimsy" (Rushdie). The distinctiveness of "magical realism", for Rushdie, is its tone of voice, "a precise note between sweetness and bitterness, the gentle acceptance of fate and anger about it". Ambiguity is the lifeblood of great art, but here it is heightened in the ability to "approach the truth by wilder, more interesting routes"; its antecedents can be found in the work of some Western authors such as Dickens, Kafka, Faulkner, stretching back to Homer

---

[52] Rushdie's best known work is "*Midnight's Children*", springing from the independence of India after British colonial rule in 1947 and its partition into two states, India and Pakistan.

and Shakespeare (Rushdie). We have seen it in the "fabulism" of African writers like Achebe and Gyasi. As an "alternate tradition" to naturalist discourse, we celebrate that "the world is not one thing but many, not singular but multiform, not constant but infinitely malleable"(Rushdie).

To read the stories of Marquez, Allende and Rushdie is to dissolve into the magical alchemy of humanity.

Listening Experience: Scheherazade (Nikolai Rimsky-Korsakov). Vienna Philharmonic; Valeri Gergiev, conductor.
www.youtube.com/watch?v=SQNymNaTr-Y&t=1228s
March 4, 2012. Accessed: 5.4.2021

Another glorious tradition of storytelling stems from the *Arabian Nights*. In this symphonic masterpiece, brilliantly conducted by Valeri Gergiev, the Russian composer Rimsky-Korsakov (1844-1908) revels in the story telling skills of Scheherazade, which saved her from execution at the hands of the capricious Sultan. We follow the tales of the Sea and Sinbad's ship, the Kalander Prince, the Young Prince and Princess, the Festival at Baghdad, and the Shipwreck, as the wrathful tones of the Sultan are subdued by the plaintive but persuasive sounds of Scheherazade. Softness and the orchestrated magic of music and stories always outlast the temporary sway of power and tyranny.

The expressive instinct: from cradle to stage

As Isabel Allende reminds us, humans are a gregarious lot. From the happy babbling of infants to the powerful oratory of professionals, we delight in giving and receiving sounds that connect us in threads of intimacy and profound insight. These are the stories that transport us from our earliest moorings to the catharsis of identity and empathy with characters who capture our deepest longings and moments of clarity amidst the tumult of everyday life. With Covid, we felt an intense loss in the absence of the performing stage, but could reflect back on incredible experiences and anticipate a thrilling return to the theatre after the pandemic.

Three stalwarts convey their encounters with Shakespeare, the incomparable bard of the English stage. Dame Judi Dench tells us "I've been mad about Shakespeare since I was about seven…*Twelfth Night* is my favourite Shakespeare, followed closely by *Measure for Measure*. The *Merchant of Venice* is probably the one I like the least. It's very difficult to make those people real, when they all behave so badly at the end. They behave quite badly at the beginning too. And a favourite line? "My bounty is as boundless as the sea, my love as deep," from *Romeo and Juliet*". (*Talking…*)

Dame Judi earned her spurs from other Shakespearean greats: "We had a famous first night (of *Henry VIII)* when all of them dried. Nobody could remember a word. Ralph Richardson had a good way of covering up if he dried on a word — he would just put the syllables in. He would go, "Ye elves of hills, brooks, standing lakes and deeeeee" instead of "groves". Almost like he was bleeping out the word… Anyway, *Henry VIII* was fine after that first night, and it was extraordinary to see (Sir John) Gielgud and Dame Edith (Evans) up close. I never went back to my dressing room; I just came off and watched. It was a masterclass every night. Until the production toured Europe, at least. On the first night in Paris I was sitting at the feet of Dame Edith as Queen Catherine. She came on, sat and missed the chair. The lights went up and all you could hear was Dame Edith saying, *Fermez la lumière*! ("put off the lights!").

Projecting the voice to enfold the audience is the paramount skill for a thespian: "A really thrilling time was in 1987, when I did *Antony and Cleopatra* with Tony Hopkins at the National Theatre. When people said, "What are you playing next?" and I said, "Cleopatra", they would roar with laughter. Outright rudeness! But we had such a good time doing it with Peter Hall at the Olivier. It was before everybody was miked so it was very good for projection. You really had to think about the person sitting on the back row of the upper circle. It was a glorious time". (*Talking...*)

True to the spirit of theatre in Shakespeare's time, social class is no barrier to entering the world of stage performance, nudged along by an inspiring mentor. As Patrick Stewart recalls, "Cecil Dormand, the English teacher at my secondary modern in West Yorkshire, was the first to put a copy of Shakespeare into my hand. We didn't have books at home. Mr Dormand went around the classroom dropping copies of *The Merchant of Venice* on desks and casting the characters. He finally said: "Stewart, you're Shylock. Start reading." There was silence while all of us read and he yelled out: "**Not to yourselves, you idiots! This is drama. It's life. Read it out aloud**." So when Shylock made his entrance, that was the first time that I ever spoke Shakespeare. No supporting roles for me!

When I was preparing to leave school, Mr Dormand stopped me one day in the corridor and said: "Stewart, have you ever considered being a professional actor?" Well, of course I hadn't. I was the son of a soldier and a weaver. Nobody from my background went into acting. But he planted the seed". (*Talking...*)

The kernel bore fruit in Stewart's career: "About ten years later, in 1966, I had my audition for the RSC[53]. I walked on to the huge, empty Stratford stage. Sitting up front were Peter Hall, John Barton and Morris Daniels, the two directors and head of casting. They asked what I was going to do... I did my piece of *Henry V*. And then John came up to the stage, lent across and said: "All right. What about trying this?" He gave me a completely different idea for the speech. I thought: "Oh Lord, I'll have a go." I did it again, and then Peter came up and said: "Very good. What about if you did it this way?" Suddenly the penny dropped. They know I can act, but can I take direction? What a revelation that was. So

---

[53] The Royal Shakespeare Company

I embraced Peter's idea, went for it 100 per cent and was offered a place in the company. Two months later I began my 15 years of work with the RSC. I'd had no education. I'd done very little Shakespeare and I hadn't mixed with intellectuals". (*Talking…*)

The creative endeavour brings expansion in multiple, and sometimes unexpected, ways. For Harriet Walter, "Shakespeare makes you reach into the depths of yourself as well as creating another character. A part is like a person we once met, grew to know, became intimately enmeshed with and finally moved away from. Some remain friends, others are like ex-lovers with whom we no longer have anything in common. All of them bring out something in us that will never go back in the books…You don't have to love everything about your characters. I hope I haven't got a lot in common with Lady Macbeth, and I don't really like Cleopatra. She is this absolute siren, with voluptuous feminine wiles, grasping at her past like Gloria Swanson getting out her old reviews. All things I'm not really keen on. But then you play it and you find you've got those qualities now. I remember saying, "Oh, how on earth am I meant to play infinite variety?" And we decided that you did it by playing each element one by one". (*Talking…*)

Director John Barton of the Royal Shakespeare Company sums up the enchantment of our experience with theatre, a sense of completion: "(he) liked to see a character's traits as beads on a necklace, and the audience as the thread joining them together". (*Talking…*)

Another powerful engagement of discourse and audience arises from the tradition of debate. Whether in the rough and tumble of a political melee, passionate contention on ethical dilemmas, or the rigorous training of Buddhist monks, the mind must confront diverse perspectives and the ability to understand (if not accept) a viewpoint that may diverge from our own[54]. Although debate may, on occasion, confirm existing assumptions, at its best it strives toward synthesis; a shrinking of the

---

[54] The French Enlightenment thinker Voltaire is credited with the classic statement: "I disagree with every word you said, but will defend with my life your right to say it".

ego, and an appeal to higher principles than narrow self-interest. It is the lynchpin of our modern democracies, as they strive for more inclusive and just polities. Here speech and civility coalesce in a pleasing and helpful evolution of thought and action.

Viewing Experience: *The Great Debaters* **(director: Denzel Washington, 2007). Excerpt.**
https://www.youtube.com/watch?v=-3wxBJ9v7qM
October 17, 2011. Accessed: 6.4.2021.

Based partly on historical fact, the debate team from the black Wiley College in Texas, James Farmer Jnr. and Samantha Booke, challenged Harvard University in the National Championship in 1935, inspired by their professor Melvin Tolson (played by Denzel Washington). Layers of history, social injustice, and race relations in America enter the arguments on both sides to the resolution that "civil disobedience is a moral right in the fight for justice". Farmer and Booke reference the Indian independence movement from British colonial rule and Gandhi's adoption of a non-violent non-cooperation movement in response to the massacre of almost 400 civilians ordered by General Dyer at Amritsar in 1919. The Harvard team counters that "non-violence is the mask that civil disobedience uses to conceal its true face – anarchy". They also argue that citizens in a democracy cannot decide which rules to obey or ignore, "nothing that erodes the rule of law can be moral". Farmer points out that black people were being lynched in Texas and there was no rule of law in the Southern United States, where blacks were denied access to schools and hospitals. He declares to the audience that "I have a duty to resist, with violence or civil disobedience: you should pray that I choose the latter".

The victory of the Wiley College team in the debate was a milestone in American education and prescient in the emergence of the civil rights movement for racial equality in the 1960's led by Martin Luther King, influenced by Gandhi and his tactics of non-violent civil disobedience. Despite notable progress in race relations in the U.S. in the last 80 years, including the election of a black President, it is remarkable that the arguments used in "The Great Debaters" extended their shadow in the "Black Lives Matter" movement in 2020. The struggle for racial equity carries on, and so does the debate on how society can continue to evolve toward outcomes that are more humane and just for all civilians. Similar to all creative endeavours, democracy is a work in motion which thrives on diverse voices.

Can Creativity Be Taught?

" You cannot teach a man anything, you can only help him find it within himself".

Galileo Galilei

Rod Judkins, an English artist, writer and lecturer on creative thinking, tells us that "at school, creativity was suppressed and crushed" (Judkins 1). This unfortunate scenario seems to play out worldwide, especially in the middle and high school years, as children are robbed of a joyous instinct and sacrificed at the altar of standardized grades, exams, and direct instruction. Since we have now entered an era of rapid change, driven by innovation and technological disruption, these educational systems must be considered anomalies. Educator, Sir Ken Robinson, argues that spawning the creative talent of students requires steps of enabling, encouragement, opportunity, inspiration and mentoring by teachers[55]. He defines creative thinking as "a process of nurturing original ideas that have value" (Robinson). As a "process", creativity can be fostered in an enabling environment, which Treffinger outlines in the steps of "generating ideas, digging deeper into ideas, openness and courage to explore ideas, and listening to one's inner voice" (in Lucas and Spencer 18).

---

[55] We saw an example of this with the Angklung Orchestra in Indonesia on page 142.

Bill Lucas and Ellen Spencer from the Centre for Real-World Learning identify five learnable dimensions or habits that would enhance the "inner voice": inquisitive, imaginative, disciplined, collaborative, and persistent (23). They use several examples of schools that have stimulated an "ecology of creative thinking"; David Harrington describes the elements to include "opportunities for play, experimentation and exploration; exciting or unusual contexts used for learning; opportunities for critical reflection that is supportive and formative; respect for difference and for others' creativity" (in Lucas and Spencer 40). We are building upon and reinforcing the child's innate curiosity, eagerness to explore the world, and to play with others. Mihaly Csikszentmihalyi sums up the emotional delights of personal creativity, which "may not lead to fame and fortune, (but) can do something that from the individual's point of view is even more important: make day-to-day experiences more vivid, more enjoyable, and more rewarding" (29).

As an educator, I find it vital to remove the "myth of creativity", which privileges the masterpieces of great artists, musicians, writers, and architects through the ages, and intimidates young minds into a belief that they lack creative talent. The creative process, in fact, applies across all subject areas (including scientific experiments and mathematical analysis) and it is a universal inheritance. Amongst the most empowering aspects of creativity is the individual student's ability to form and develop a viewpoint on issues of contemporary relevance, refined in dialogue and discussion with peers and teachers. **It becomes the springboard for the emergence of a mental map that will guide beliefs and actions in adult life**[56]. As Galileo reminds us, the goal of education is for each person to discover their unique voice and sense of agency in the world. That is the true magic of the creative instinct.

---

[56]   In terms of Robinson's definition of creative thinking, nothing could be of greater value.

Expansive Space: Resonating Walls, Domes, and Pillars

The ecology of creative thinking emerges from multiple sources, as mentors at home and beyond build upon our biological inclination of wonder and exploration. A fertile fount in history can be traced to the faith traditions that enriched civilizations and founded communities united in belief and practice. The requirement of a collective space sparked the construction and adornment of magnificent temples, churches, synagogues, and mosques that have resonated with sounds of worship and guidance through the ages. Architecture in the Islamic world is particularly striking, given the rapid spread of the religion and consolidation of political power after its founding in the 7th century C.E. Within seven centuries, Islamic empires and communities stretched from Spain in Southern Europe to China, from Arabia and Persia to large parts of Africa, the Indian subcontinent, and Southeast Asia[57]. Apart from mosques and monastic halls, the buildings in this vast area included schools, hospitals, military fortifications, political assemblies, palaces, markets, and mausoleums. Contrary to the assumption of Islam as a monolithic faith and culture, its architecture reveals a marvellous ability to adapt to local environments, reflected also in a colourful variation of practices and customs. Even in its originating sphere in West Asia, it was exposed to the influence of Roman, Byzantine, and Sassanid civilizations (al Kadi). The magnificent Alhambra in Granada, Andalusia (southern Spain), a jewel of the Islamic Moors, carries the imprint of Roman arches, domes, and fountains[58]. In West Africa, Senegal and Mali mosques with conical towers preserve local traditions of mud architecture. Samarkand and Bukhara in Uzbekistan continue to dazzle with the glow of the ancient Silk Road, their walls and towers seeped with the hues of exchange, of material and spiritual

---

[57] The Southeast Asian nation of Indonesia is now the largest Islamic country, with about 85% of its population of 260 million following the Muslim faith.

[58] The sound of water from concealed canals as one climbs the hill toward the entrance of the Alhambra is a truly enchanting experience, anticipating the earthly paradise within its walls.

fulfilment. The Mughal rulers in India commanded a fusion of marble and red sandstone, enhanced by the intricate skills of local artisans, to compose buildings of eternal charm. The prayer halls in Malaysia and Indonesia conserve the layered stability and majestic contours of tropical timber. The uniting elements across continents are intricate geometrical patterns, including the ravishing three-dimensional "muqarnas" ornamental vaults (al Kadi), and the aesthetic flourish of calligraphy sustaining sacred voices from scripture[59]. From artistic and cultural angles, it would be more appropriate to use the term "Islams" (with similar plurals for all faith traditions), conveying the joyous plurality of lived experience amidst the commonality of belief. Even in this most intimate inner space, humans thrive with creative diversity.

"Muqarnas" and calligraphy at the Alhambra Palace, Granada, Spain (credit: Ali, Zirrar).

---

[59] These elements dominated Islamic religious architecture, given the prohibition of the depiction of living beings, human or animal, in sacred spaces, since that was considered *"shirk"* or competing with the Creator.

Evening Prayer, Mosque at the Taj Mahal, Agra, India (credit: author).

Sakhi Zinda (mausoleum), Samarkand, Uzbekistan. (credit: Arun Taneja)

The Orchestra of the Brain: Sounds of Pleasure

"Music is a higher revelation than all wisdom and philosophy"

Ludwig van Beethoven

Of all the expressive arts, language and music seem to have arisen as agreeable companions from the beginning of the human journey. They perhaps imbibed together from the stream of natural sound, ranging from animal calls to bird song, creating moments of deep pleasure amidst the imitation and tasks of survival. Dan Levitin from McGill University[60] tells us that "music is unusual among all human activities for both its *ubiquity* and its *antiquity*. No known human culture now or anytime in the recorded past lacked music. Some of the oldest human artifacts found in human and protohuman excavation sites are musical instruments: bone flutes and animal skins stretched over tree stumps to make drums...for most of human history, music making was as natural an activity as breathing and walking, and everyone participated" (Levitin 5-6). Modern neuroscience unveiled a compelling clue for the universal appeal of music: unlike previous ideas of language and the arts inhabiting the left and right hemispheres of our brain respectively, brain scans show with clarity that music radiates much beyond a limited sphere. Musical activity "involves nearly every region of the brain that we know about, and nearly every neural subsystem" (Levitin 85-86).

For example, when we hear the Piano Concerto no. 3 by Russian composer Rachmaninov (1873-1943), " the hair cells in my cochlea parse the incoming sounds into different frequency bands, sending electrical signals to my primary auditory cortex...telling it what frequencies are present in the signal. Additional regions in the temporal lobe, including the superior temporal sulcus and the superior temporal gyrus on both

---

[60] He holds the James McGill Chair in Psychology and runs the Laboratory for Musical Perception, Cognition and Expertise at McGill University in Montreal, Canada.

sides of the brain, help to distinguish the different timbres I'm hearing[61]. If I want to label those timbres, the hippocampus helps to retrieve the memory of similar sounds I've heard before, and then I'll need to access my mental dictionary – which will require using structures found at the junction between the temporal, occipital, and parietal lobes… Whole new populations of neurons will become active as I attend to pitch sequences (dorsolateral prefrontal cortex, and Brodmann areas 44 and 47), rhythms (the lateral cerebellum and the cerebellar vermis), and emotion (frontal lobes, cerebellum, the amygdala and the nucleus accumbens)– part of a network of structures involved in feelings of pleasure and reward" (Levitin 91). Dopamine, the "feel good" neurochemical, is released particularly in the phase of anticipation of the flow and pattern of the piece, accompanied with a lowering of cortisol, the "stress hormone" (Harvey). Music brings together the cognitive and emotional wiring in the brain, accompanied with rapture. In other words, the brain conducts its own melodious orchestra. No wonder Deanna Choi from Queen's University claims that music may be better for you than chocolate and sex! (Choi).

Listening Experience 1: Rachmaninov Piano Concerto no. 3. Vladimir Horowitz (pianist), New York Philharmonic Orchestra, conductor Zubin Mehta.
https://www.youtube.com/watch?v=D5mxU_7BTRA
January 25, 2009. Accessed: 11.4.2021

This was the last recording of the concerto in 1978 by Horowitz, considered among the greatest pianists of the 20th century. He conveys every nuance of emotion in this stunning work, which ranges from sorrowful pathos to playful variation to exuberant jubilation. The finale will sweep you off your feet.

---

[61] Timbre refers to the tonal colours which help us to distinguish between instruments as well as the range of sounds within an instrument.

Replicating our musical adventure as a species, there are good reasons to caress it as a loving accompaniment throughout our lives. Taking advantage of the unbridled plasticity of the young brain, early musical training shapes changes in the brain structure and the formation of new pathways that have positive and long term impacts on cognitive and social performance, including literacy and reasoning skills. An enhanced cortical thickness in musicians boosts the ability of the frontal cortex in tasks of executive planning and anticipation (Zattore). **This makes a strong case for the inclusion of musical education in all school curricula** (Collins). At the other end of the age spectrum, the therapeutic benefits of music become evident in the treatment of patients with dementia or recovery from stroke and Parkinson's disease. Motor performance is seen to improve for movement impairment, and the evocative nature of music elicits memories for those sliding toward amnesia and Alzheimer's. The emotional valence of song and melody may help in retaining or even regaining neural connections and a better mental focus (Harvey, Choi).

Music reproduces the comfort of early parental attachment in the release of oxytocin, our love hormone, which reduces fear and nourishes trust and social bonding. Inclusive, ensemble singing and playing of instruments was the norm in indigenous cultures and most pre-industrial societies, learned in childhood and secured in adulthood. Whereas language is an "individualizer", in the exchange of talking and listening, music is the "harmonizer", the bridge to a more connected world (Harvey). No other creative impulse has enriched us to the same extent as this "Oxytocin feast", which we can reap generously for infinite euphoria.

Listening Experience 2: The Best of Opera[62]
https://www.youtube.com/watch?v=g4LOpDVkzD0
November 13, 2014. Accessed: 13.4.2021

---

[62] The selections here are from Western, primarily European, opera. Others may find it interesting to explore musical and theatrical traditions like Chinese opera.

Exult with six hours of the human voice as it glides through every conceivable range, pitch and sonority and the entire panoply of emotion. The voice is our greatest gift from nature, and composers through the ages have lifted our spirits beyond words into an ineffable realm. The Italians greet each other before an opera performance with "Si diverti", "have fun". This is enjoyment on an operatic scale indeed!

The "best of opera" collection transports us into rapture with the masterpieces of the Italian, French, and German greats, from Verdi and Puccini to Bizet and Wagner to the incomparable Mozart. Legendary singers (paired as female and male) Callas and Pavarotti, Sutherland and Domingo, Nilsson and Caruso, Flagstad and Bocelli, Fleming and Lanza, Norman and Carreras, Price and Wunderlich, Te Kanawa and Corelli, Bartoli and Kraus, Damrau and Gobbi, Horne and Vickers – one must anticipate a lifetime of soaring elation and "goose bumps" in stepping into an exuberant elixir.

**Listening Experience 3: *Da Tempeste* ("from the tempest to bliss").
G.F. Handel (1685-1759).**
Amanda Forsyth, soprano. Cleveland Baroque Orchestra.
https://www.youtube.com/watch?v=6xzcgWOod-U
June 18, 2014. Accessed: 20.3.2021

Apart from Handel's uplifting music and the brilliant range of Amanda Forsyth's artistry, this song has a particular resonance in our struggle through the dark times of Covid:

> *When the ship, broken by storms,*
> *Succeeds at last in making it to port,*
> *It no longer knows what it desires.*
> *Thus, the heart, after torments and woes,*
> *Once it recovers its solace,*
> *Is beside itself with bliss.*
> (translated from Italian).

Even in the depths of despair, this music restores the balm of a healing touch.

Listening Experience 4: The *Magic Flute* and Other Wonders from Mozart

"5 minutes that will make you love Mozart"

(New York Times, Arts and Culture; December 14, 2020).

"I think few human bodies have brought as much joy to the world as Mozart".

Ragnar Kjartansson, Icelandic artist

"Mozart is life itself".

Colin Davis, English conductor

In a brief lifespan of 35 years, Wolfgang Amadeus Mozart (1756-91) gifted the world a creative outpouring of astonishing variety and genius. His story was equally staggering, moving from child prodigy to the favoured performer in aristocratic and royal courts to rejection for his daring compositions and an early death due to illness and poverty. His music, not surprisingly, strikes every note and nuance of emotion. As the New York Times critic David Allen writes, " So much of what I love about Mozart tends toward the poignant: his ability to express both the pain and beauty of the human condition, the way his music 'smiles through the tears,' as the musicologist H.C. Robbins Landon put it. But he also offers moments of pure, unbridled joy" (*5 Minutes…*).

This collection from the New York Times is an excellent introduction to Mozart's oeuvre, with extracts from opera arias, concertos, serenades, sonatas and the heartrending Requiem, which foreshadowed his death and was left incomplete. Each piece is an invitation to delve further into music of endless wonder and pleasure. The finale from Act 1 of the *"Magic Flute"* opera offers a taster for the rampaging "Queen of the Night" aria, which tests any singer's vocal calisthenics, and the dulcet romantic duets of Papageno and Papagena. One of my favourite songs in all music is the trio *"Soave sia il vento"* from Mozart's opera *"Cosi fan tutte"*. Dutch conductor, Bernard Haitink calls it "one of the most sublime things I know. The text is *'May the winds be gentle, and the sea calm'*, and you can almost feel the breezes gently blowing and the waves lapping in the sound of the violins as it starts. Such beauty, tenderness and longing, all in the space of just over two and a half minutes". *(5 minutes…).* The brilliant Japanese pianist Dame Mitsuko Uchida says this song "brings tears to my eyes every time the strings start playing" *(5 Minutes…).* If art reaches toward perfection, Mozart brings us ever closer to those truly exalted moments.

Listening Experience 5: From the Beatles to Beyonce

The Beatles – Greatest Hits[63]
https://www.youtube.com/watch?v=ukhpsC7Nng0
August 17, 2020. Accessed: 12.4.2021

Beyonce – *Black Parade* (Grammy winner 2021)
https://www.youtube.com/watch?v=EJT1m1ele00
June 20, 2020. Accessed: 14.4.2021

Every art form shines a light on the cultural and historical context of its time of creation. The greatest art transcends time and transmits a universal spirit. The songs of the Beatles throb with the breath and vitality of the 1960's, a decade pulsating with the calls for liberation, both personal and sexual, the struggle for equality, and the demands for peace

---

[63] Aficionados will always opt for their *Sgt. Pepper's Lonely Hearts Club Band,* considered the greatest rock album of all time.

rather than war. Their songs tugged the heart strings of romance for both young and old, but also became the rallying cry for a generation that challenged the prevailing norms and values of the ruling class predicated on material consumption and military force. Beyonce's songs confirm the unfinished agenda from, not just the last six decades, but rooted even deeper in history – the discrimination against people of African descent and their continued striving for equal rights and justice. She won an astonishing and record breaking 28th. Grammy award in 2021 for "*Black Parade*", mingling calls for reparation for historical wrongs with a celebration of black pride and its moorings in a rich ancestry.

Black Parade
(extracts)

I'm goin' back to the South
I'm goin' back, back, back, back
Where my roots ain't watered down
Growin', growin' like a Baobab tree….
Ooh, melanin, melanin, my drip is skin deep, like
Ooh, motherland, motherland, motherland, drip on me
Eeya, I can't forget my history is her story, yeah
Being black, maybe that's the reason why they always mad Yeah, they always mad, yeah
Been passed 'em, I know that's the reason why they all big mad
And they always have been
Honey, come around my way,
around my hive

Whenever momma says so, momma says so
Here I come on my throne, sittin' high
Follow my parade, oh, my parade…
We got rhythm, we got pride
We birth kings, we birth tribes

Holy river, holy tongue
Speak the glory, feel the love
Motherland, motherland drip on me, hey, hey, hey.

The songs of the Beatles and Beyonce, just as those of countless other musical artists, ensure that the voice remains the supreme instrument of human inspiration and fulfilment.

Listening Experience 6: "My life would be meaningless without music" – the Landfill Harmonic from Cateura, Paraguay

The world sends us garbage, we send back music. Favio Chavez, TedX Amsterdam
https://www.youtube.com/watch?v=CsfOvJEdurk
November 8, 2013. Accessed: 14.4.2021

Landfill Harmonic – the "Recycled Orchestra"
https://www.youtube.com/watch?v=yYbORpgSmjg
November 7, 2013. Accessed: 14.4.2021

Music is such an indelible human impulse that it can surface in even the most unimaginable circumstances. The Landfill Harmonic was birthed in a slum of garbage recycling workers in Cateura, Paraguay. The inhabitants turn the trash in their midst into musical instruments, a brilliant blend of creativity and ecology. The violin is constructed from paint cans, wood pallets, a baking tray for pizza and a fork, and similar ingenuity generates woodwinds and drums as part of the "Recycled Orchestra". An eleven year old violinist says that "when I listen to the sound of a violin, I feel butterflies in my stomach", a sentiment echoed by seasoned professionals and audiences worldwide. The values of this orchestra go beyond the music; as one of the performers remarks poignantly, "people realize we shouldn't throw away trash… well, we shouldn't throw away people either". Music restores dignity and grace to these young souls.

When it comes time to perform, the Harmonia chooses none other than Mozart and his charming "Eine Kleine Nachtmusik" ("*A Little Night Music*"). A girl from the orchestra expresses a feeling that is universal and eternal: "my life would be meaningless without music".

Listening Experience 7: Heavenly Sounds
Tibetan Monks – multiphonic chanting
https://www.youtube.com/watch?v=1pkNZCZaxiM
March 5, 2013. Accessed: 22.3.2021

When the venerable American scholar of world religions, Huston Smith, visited a Tibetan monastery in 1965, he was startled to hear a sound from the chanting *lamas* (monks) that he had never encountered before. He discerned a first, third and barely audible fifth tone in a single voice, which was then magnified by the chanting choir. He called it "the holiest sound I'd ever heard" (Smith). On his return to America, sound scientists at MIT[64] identified it as an unusual mode of "multiphonic chanting", which amplifies the overtones[65]. Smith saw this music as an elevating form of worship, whose purpose is "to shift from peripheral to focal awareness the mystery and wonder of the world" (Smith). When we reach a state of meditative focus, all distinction between the deity, *lama*, and sound disappears. Music sweeps us along the wave of deepest realization and inner harmony.

Sources/Citations

Al Kadi, Rana. *"In Pursuit of Heritage: Tracing the early elements of Islamic architecture"*. (Library of Congress).
https://www.youtube.com/watch?v=b28OKGImVuA
April 25, 2017. Accessed: 10.4.2021

---

[64] Massachusetts Institute of Technology
[65] Similar forms of "multiphonic" or "polyphonic" sounds, sometimes referred to as "throat singing", have been identified in other parts of Central Asia, Africa, and Native American cultures.

A Long Petal of the Sea, Isabel Allende.
https://www.youtube.com/watch?v=zWgvS0rXR58
January 24, 2020. Accessed: 4.4.2021

Adichie, Chimamanda Ngozi. *"The Danger of a Single Story".*
https://www.youtube.com/watch?v=D9Ihs241zeg
October 8, 2009. Accessed: 6.4.2021

Ali, Zirrar. *"Muqarnas: Honeycomb architecture that touches the heavens".*
Middle East Eye, April 27, 2020.

Allende, Isabel. 2020. *A Long Petal of the Sea.* Bloomsbury, London.

Choi, Deanna. "How music can be better for you than sex and chocolate".
www.youtube.com/watch?v=XZFKpkDUMB4&t=1s
December 15, 2012. Accessed: 29.8.2020

Collins, Anita. *What if every child had access to music education from birth?*
https://www.youtube.com/watch?v=ueqgenARzlE
October 28, 2014. Accessed: 10.4.2021

Eagleman, David. *"The Creative Brain"*
https://www.youtube.com/watch?v=8tN3J_V-J5w
May 29, 2018. Accessed: 31.3.2021

5 Minutes that will make you love Mozart. The New York Times (Arts and Ideas). December 14, 2020.

Gyasi, Yaa. *Homegoing* (Chicago Humanities Festival).
https://www.youtube.com/watch?v=LoEAWvTvFus&t=1s
December 6, 2016. Accessed: 2.4.2021

Half of a Yellow Sun, Chimamanda Ngozi Adichie.
https://www.youtube.com/watch?v=_NsELe67UxM
May 31, 2020. Accessed: 7.4.2021

Harjo, Joy, ed. 2020. *When the Light of the World was Subdued, our Songs Came Through* (Native Nations Poetry).
W.W. Norton, New York.

Harvey, Alan. *Your Brain on Music*
https://www.youtube.com/watch?v=MZFFwy5fwYI
June 27, 2018. Accessed: 12.8.2020

Judkins, Rod. 2015. *The Art of Creative Thinking.* Sceptre, London.

Levitin, Daniel. 2006. *This Is Your Brain On Music.* Atlantic Books, London.

Lucas, Bill and Spencer, Ellen. 2017. *Teaching Creative Thinking.* Crown House, Wales.

Patke, Rajeev S. 2006. *Postcolonial Poetry in English.* Oxford U Press.

Robinson, Sir Ken. "*Can Creativity Be Taught?*"
https://www.youtube.com/watch?v=vlBpDggX3iE
August 30, 2014. Accessed: 15.4.2021

Rushdie, Salman. *Gabriel Garcia Marquez Symposium*, Univ. of Texas, Austin (opening keynote).
https://www.youtube.com/watch?v=TtxK_y5cBcw
October 31, 2015. Accessed: 7.4.2021

Smith, Huston. "*The Wisdom of Faith*" (Hinduism and Buddhism).
www.youtube.com/watch?v=GDmCso3-sac&t=2259s
September 29, 2017. Accessed: 15.4.2021

"*Talking Shakespeare*". The London Times, August 7, 2020.

Viet Thanh Nguyen. "Narrative Plenitude" (Google Talks).
https://www.youtube.com/watch?v=gqiPoZOy3VE&t=1s
December 19, 2018. Accessed: 22.10.2020

Zattore, Robert. "*From Perception to Pleasure: How Music Changes Your Brain*".
https://www.youtube.com/watch?v=KVX8j5s53Os&t=4s
April 12, 2018. Accessed: 20.8.2020

The Sixth Circle of Joy

The creative energy unleashed in the fifth circle discovers a source of substantial amplification in the sixth, centred at the pineal gland. As the "inner eye", this circle combines external stimulus and internal insight in an expansion with endless possibilities. In the earlier circles, we had celebrated the movement of the body and now we exalt **the movement of the mind**, scaling heights and pushing boundaries in an exploration without restraint. Reality is pierced, then stretched and extended in directions which offer often startling new vistas and visions. This is a fun and enthralling encounter, in consonance with our age of bustling innovation.

Lateral thinking opens the mind with divergent and challenging perspectives. We may not only enjoy decoding puzzling conundrums, but also confront issues of social and cultural concern, ranging from mental health to the construction of inclusive communities and policies. The generation and exchange of ideas spawn inventive solutions. Artists marry their intuition or "gut instinct" from the third circle with refined technique and skill to transform our engagement with the world and to stir our inner landscapes as well. Music takes on the quality of playful variation and infinite delight, the sounds entering orbits of vibration deep within our being.

Appropriately, **design** can be seen as a metaphor for our times, integrating ideas from diverse subject areas and combining aesthetics with utility. It has become a pervasive presence in the products we admire and consume, the buildings that grace a pleasing urbanism, the devices connecting us across vast swathes of time and space, the flourishes of imagination that leave us in wonder. The historical record, though, reminds us that the designer instinct has always been a magnet for humans, elevating the ability to shape the external environment with innate foresight and tactile prowess. When we begin to shape our own lives in pleasing contours, design comes home as an amiable companion.

Among the challenges of living in an insistently inventive and speedy time period, distractibility and the lack of focused attention could drive a spiralling disorientation. The "third eye" restores the *yinyang* equilibrium of activity and stillness. Meditative contemplation renews calmness and tranquillity. In the lower circles, we moved the breath in skilful energization. Now, we lengthen and soften our breath in composure.

The synthesis of focus and insight at this circle anticipates the culminating fulfilment at the next.

Lateral thinking: the movement of the mind

> "Rightness is what matters in vertical thinking. Richness is what matters in lateral thinking".
>
> Edward De Bono

De Bono, who may be considered the "guru" of lateral thinking, considers its basic principle to be "that any particular way of looking at things is only one from among many other possible ways". (De Bono 58). It is quite distinct from the more "traditional" form taught in most school settings or "vertical thinking" which "moves forward by sequential steps each of which must be justified"[66] (11), and usually results in confirmation of existing concepts and information. Lateral thinking, also referred to in common parlance as "thinking outside the box", attempts to be deliberately

---

[66] This is also seen as a distinction between "convergent" (vertical) and "divergent" (lateral) thinking; the former converges toward a conclusion, often formulaic, while the latter promotes multiple possibilities.

provocative and challenging, since "it is concerned with breaking out of the concept prisons of old ideas…(and) with the generation of new ideas" (11). This makes it consonant with the needs of restless innovation in our times, the hunger for new ideas that "are the stuff of change and progress in every field from science to art, from politics to personal happiness" (11).

It is important to recognize that lateral thinking is not purely disruptive; rather it "stimulates new pattern formation by juxtaposing unlikely information" (51), making it an active ally of creativity and problem solving. As a process and a learnable skill, several strategies may be employed including brainstorming, idea generation, focus tools, and "disproof thinking" (questioning previous assumptions with the notion that "the majority is always wrong"). More significantly, lateral thinking nurtures a habit and attitude "that tempers the arrogance of any rigid conclusion…of (inflexibility) and dogma" (49). The mind is freed from hasty judgement and from the constraints of conditioned learning, and it "moves for the sake of moving" (38). The movement is accompanied by pleasurable expansion of our neural pathways.

Learning Activity - Part A: Lateral Puzzles (for all ages)

The excitement in lateral thinking is to generate as many alternative approaches as possible. Even if we arrive at one "solution" that seems the most satisfying, none of the other possibilities may be discounted – the process is more important than any outcome. The lateral puzzles that follow will certainly keep people of any age engaged in thinking "outside the box", and it's more fun when the class or group bounce ideas off each other!

Puzzle 1. The Man in the Elevator[67]

A man lives on the tenth floor of a building. Every day he takes the elevator to go down to the ground floor to go to work or to go shopping.

---

[67] Source for puzzles 1-6: http://www.techinterviewpuzzles.com/2010/06/paul-sloanes-list-of-classic-lateral.html (accessed 20.5.2020)

When he returns he takes the elevator to the seventh floor and walks up the stairs to reach his apartment on the tenth floor. He hates walking so why does he do it?

Puzzle 2. The Man who Hung Himself

Not far from Madrid, there is a large wooden barn. The barn is completely empty except for a dead man hanging from the middle of the central rafter. The rope around his neck is ten feet long and his feet are three feet off the ground. The nearest wall is 20 feet away from the man. It is not possible to climb up the walls or along the rafters. The man hanged himself. How did he do it?

Puzzle 3. Anthony and Cleopatra

Anthony and Cleopatra are lying dead on the floor of a villa in Egypt. Nearby is a broken bowl. There is no mark on either of their bodies and they were not poisoned. How did they die?

Puzzle 4. Trouble with Sons

A woman had two sons who were born on the same hour of the same day of the same year. But they were not twins. How could this be so?

Puzzle 5. Push that Car

A woman pushed her car. She stopped when she reached a hotel at which point, she knew she was bankrupt. Why?

Puzzle 6. Heaven

A woman died and went to Heaven. There were thousands of other people there. They were all naked and all looked as they did at the age of 21. She looked around to see if there was anyone she recognized. She saw a couple and knew immediately that they were Adam and Eve. How did she know?

Puzzle 7: Coconut Millionaire[68]

A man buys coconuts at $5 a dozen and sells them at $3 a dozen. Because of this he becomes a millionaire. How?

Part B: "Koans" from Zen Buddhism (older students and adults)

Koans are paradoxical puzzles used in Zen Buddhism to free the mind from rigid and fixed thinking. The practitioners move away from "traditional" step-by-step logic toward a more intuitive understanding. Sharing the qualities of lateral thinking, the explanations given may be understood at multiple levels.

Koan 1: A Cup of Tea

Nan-in, a Japanese master during the Meiji era (1868-1912), received a university professor who came to inquire about Zen. Nan-in served tea. He poured his visitor's cup full, and then kept on pouring. The professor watched the overflow until he no longer could restrain himself. "It is overfull. No more will go in!" "Like this cup," Nan-in said, "you are full of your own opinions and speculations. How can I show you Zen unless you first empty your cup?"

Koan 2: Muddy Road

Tanzan and Ekido were once traveling together down a muddy road. A heavy rain was still falling. Coming around a bend, they met a lovely girl in a silk kimono and sash, unable to cross the intersection. "Come on, girl" said Tanzan at once. Lifting her in his arms, he carried her over the mud. Ekido did not speak again until that night when they reached a lodging temple. Then he no longer could restrain himself. "We monks don't go near females," he told Tanzan, "especially not young and lovely

---

[68] Source for puzzle 7: Sloane, Paul (2017).

ones. It is dangerous. Why did you do that?" "I left the girl there," said Tanzan. "Are you still carrying her"?

Koan 3: A Parable

A man traveling across a field encountered a tiger. He fled, the tiger after him. Coming to a precipice, he caught hold of the root of a wild vine and swung himself down over the edge. The tiger sniffed at him from above. Trembling, the man looked down to where, far below, another tiger was waiting to eat him. Only the vine sustained him.

Two mice, one white and one black, little by little started to gnaw away the vine. The man saw a luscious strawberry near him. Grasping the vine with one hand, he plucked the strawberry with the other. How sweet it tasted!

Koan 4: Temple Flag

Two monks were arguing about the temple flag waving in the wind.

One said, "The flag moves."

The other said, "The wind moves."

They argued back and forth but could not agree.

Hui-neng, the sixth patriarch, said: "Gentlemen! It is not the flag that moves. It is not the wind that moves. It is your mind that moves."[69]

Inclusive theatre: expanded possibilities and outcomes

I was fortunate to witness a classroom performance of improvisational theatre at Keystone Academy, Beijing, inspired by the concepts and practices

---

[69] Sources:
- https://fractalenlightenment.com/37292/spirituality/5-zen-koans-that-will-open-your-mind (accessed on 25.5.2020)
- https://thebuddhafultao.wordpress.com/2012/01/29/some-great-koans/ (accessed on 25.5.2020)

of The Theatre of the Oppressed (TOTO)[70]. Developed by the Brazilian playwright, Augusto Boal, in the 1970's and influenced by the ideas of educator, Paulo Freire, there is no separation between spectator and performer here. Audience members are encouraged, as "*spect-actors*", to explore, analyse, and transform the scenario unfolding on stage. They are asked to consider guiding questions as the performance evolves, including:

1. *What do you see?*

2. *Think and observe closely. What do you think you see? What do you really see? How do these two things differ?*

3. *How would you approach the situation portrayed on stage?*

4. *How might you make a change to improve the situation observed? How can you apply your ideas as real actions on stage?*

5. *What would you do on stage to participate and/or intervene? Which characters would be involved? Why?*

The active role of the *spect-actors* enables them to think for themselves and contribute solutions to the play's questions. The imagination and creativity of the *spect-actors* becomes central. Boal has emphasized that the goal of TOTO is not to show a single 'correct path', but rather to discover all possible paths which may be further examined. Playing different roles gives participants and performers varied perspectives in viewing reality. Lateral thinking and problem solving merge in an empowering partnership.

In the lesson that I observed, the students chose and crafted scripts on two issues of immediate concern: school bullying and mental health. The element of "group brainstorming" enabled them to construct a range of

---

[70] I am indebted to my former colleague, Joel Godiah, the High School Theatre teacher at Keystone Academy, Beijing, for the opportunity to observe his class of grade 11 (17-year- old) students and for an extended conversation that followed.

scenarios and, with the participation of the *spect-actors* (other groups), to create an active dialogue on diverse perspectives and possible solutions. However, unlike most 'traditional' theatre, there is a greater acceptance of open-ended outcomes, with social implications that echo far beyond classroom walls. Elements of "cyber bullying" and indeed "cyber warfare" have become universal concerns, as much as mental health issues of depression, anxiety, and anomie, none of which are easily tackled. Story telling in TOTO resonates with reality, since life often carries on without easy or neat conclusions.

In an animated conversation after class, we commended the students for extending the idea of "oppression" beyond the connotation of exploitation of others. It could now be viewed as a sort of "heaviness" in the mind, observed both in the internal (mental depression) and external (bullying, exclusion) spheres. A student explains the excitement of this creative experience: "It gives us more space to express our own ideas. You can make a change and address social issues; the audience can put themselves in the same situation and think about it. In traditional theatre, the audience may have many questions in their head; in this, you go on stage and make the change…For most theatre, we have to use some kind of convention; for this, you can use your own imagination and create your own ending. I really like it, it's unique". The teacher adds his joyful endorsement: "There is no one single formula, it is so expansive in nature". The process creates its own magic.

The design impulse: shaping spaces and lives

De Bono, as much as the practitioners of TOTO, remind us that lateral thinking initiates the possibility of new ideas with the capacity to transform our outlook on myriad aspects of life. Daniel Pink, author of "*A Whole New Mind*", calls the 21st century the "Conceptual Age" (Pink 49), with design emerging as the metaphor for the world emerging in our midst. Design engages different parts of the brain, being "a classic whole-minded aptitude…a combination of utility and significance" (70). In many ways, though, humans have **always** embraced design, evidenced by the astonishing range of artefacts shaped by our ancestors that pushed us toward an abundance in comfort and spirit. In 2010, the BBC Radio 4 selected 100 objects from the British Museum as a representation of world history, organized in specific periods from "Making us Human" (2,000,000 to 9,000 BCE) to "The World of Our Making" (1914 to 2010 CE). Among the earliest objects are a stone chopping tool and a volcanic rock hand axe from Olduvai in the African Rift Valley, a tribute to the first humans and their ability to remould the natural environment in ways that ensured our survival and thriving. By 9,000 BCE humans had begun the domestication of grains and animals that would transform our existence with the boon of fertility and plenty. In celebration, the bounty of nature merged with intimate desire and emotion – at a cave in Ain Sakhri in the Judean desert the dwellers carved an exquisite figurine of lovers in an embrace, carved from pebble. Creativity and romance began their intricate dance, and those steps continue to resonate today[71].

Learning Activity (for students of all ages, group activity):

BBC Radio 4 and the British Museum: A History of the World in 100 Objects
https://www.bbc.co.uk/programmes/b00nrtd2/episodes/downloads

After examining the objects presented in the podcasts by the British Museum, select ANY FOUR from different time periods that represent a major development in human history and explain their significance. Share your choices with other groups, followed with a discussion on the role of creativity in accompanying our story from the beginning.

---

[71] Perhaps none more so than in "Bollywood" popular cinema from India, song and dance fests invoking fertility and romance in equal measure.

This selection ends in 2010. Now choose an object that might best translate the events of the last decade, including the events of 2020. There are several possibilities: the handphone camera, Covid masks, video virtual communication tools, refugee boats, green energy appliances. Reflect on the possibilities of global cooperation and partnership in tackling the challenges of the present and in shaping a future with more inclusive growth and prosperity. What might future historians find the most ingenious and creative legacy of our time?

Through the ages, design has shared the affinity of lateral thinking for inter-disciplinary investigation, drawing its inspiration from multiple areas of study and cultural traditions. It has rightly reclaimed its centrality as a paradigm in our times. We can admire the beauty of design not just in architecture and technology that reshapes the environment, but also in adopting it as the architect of our own story and mindset.

Gaudi's *Sagrada Familia*: The Forest of Faith

The charming city of Barcelona envelops the visitor in the astonishing shapes and structures envisioned by Antoni Gaudi (1852-1926). Dutch scholar, Gijs van Hensbergen, asserts that Gaudi reinvented the language of architecture and marvels at "his capacity to see space in a totally different way, to see space explode" (*God's Architect*). No building exemplifies this better than the *Sagrada Familia*, which Gaudi intended as a monument to his deep Catholic faith, which is evident in the sculptures and stained glass that embellish his grand conception. However, Gaudi reached even deeper into the human spiritual treasure, turning to Nature as his greatest inspiration. He imagined the interior columns as trees reaching skywards, since "trees are actually buildings, they know where to throw out a branch" (*God's Architect*). The "branches" of stone at the *Sagrada* appear at different levels in order to support all the upper weight. Gaudi wanted to create the aura of a forest, where humans could feel intimate with the Creator. The colours bring us closer to the story of his faith, with the blue and green of the Nativity of Jesus façade in the East melding into the darker red, yellow and orange of the Passion in the setting sun.

The fusion of religious faith and nature makes the *Sagrada* a stunning expression, and it was too grand to be completed in Gaudi's lifetime! It continues to attract pilgrims from far and wide, like the Japanese sculptor Etsuko Soto, who has worked on fulfilling Gaudi's vision; for him, "Gaudi is not dead". (*God's Architect*) We must all hope for the culmination of his dream in 2026, which would mark the hundredth anniversary of his death. That would be a fitting tribute to an extraordinary universal mind and his "explosion in stone"[72].

---

[72] Photos of the *Sagrada Familia*, Barcelona, on pages 183 and 184; credit: author.

Dame Zaha Hadid: Flirtations in Space, Liberation from Gravity

The Iraqi-British designer and architect, Dame Zaha Hadid (1950-2016), saw displacement from her home country as a source of enormous freedom, blending over-lapping and fluid influences in her constructions that sweep across multiple expanses in different corners of the world. In particular, she credited the work of the Russian artist Kazimir Malevich and "Suprematism"[73] from the early 20th century in galvanizing a new form of organizing space. Architecture could create its own language of "fragmentation, flotation, and open composition" (Oxford). The viewer and the wanderer could be bewitched into experiencing a liberation from the laws of nature, gravity itself, a sublime form of suspended animation.

At the Messner Mountain Museum Corones in the Italian Tyrol, honouring the achievements of the renowned climber, Reinhold Messner[74], Hadid created the dramatic interplay of the challenges and thrills of mountaineering: "the idea is that visitors can descend within the mountain to explore its caverns and grottos, before emerging through the mountain wall on the other side, out onto the terrace overhanging the valley far below with spectacular, panoramic views" (*ArchDaily*). This Alpine vision is akin to a levitation escapade. At the Soho Wangjing in China's capital, the three curving towers conjure an interweaving mountain landscape within an urban complex. Beijing's new Daxing airport radiates with the extended arms of the starfish, Hadid recreating our amphibian origins and the timeless wanderlust that links us across the seas.

At the Heydar Aliyev Centre in Azerbaijan's capital, Baku, Hadid utilized the new material of fibre concrete in a malleable and expansive statement of pride for the Azeri nation. It was a deliberate riposte to the functional, stolid architecture imposed for seven decades by the Soviet Union upon its satellite states, and homage to the Russian avant-garde that had inspired her creative journey. With her flirtations in space, the "queen of curves" married personal freedom and the pliant earth.

---

[73] The Suprematism art movement focused on abstract geometric forms, and was influenced by Cubism and Futurism from the same time period.

[74] Messner was the first to climb all 14 mountains in the world over 8,000 meters, and the first to climb Mount Everest without the aid of tanked oxygen.

Heydar Aliyev Centre: Baku, Azerbaijan. (*worldarchitecture.org*)

Paul Andreu: The Giant Egg, Dramatic Womb

My first sighting of the National Centre for Performing Arts (NCPA) in Beijing left me mesmerized. The hemispherical apparition glinting with the rays of the setting sun, reflected in the pool of surrounding water, promised a magical encounter. Fondly called the "Giant Egg", it carried the expectation of a grand hatching, and my first steps inside did not disappoint. Looking up at the roof, we witness the flow of water, seemingly defying gravity yet carefully channelled. The aura of fertility finds its fruition in the concert halls and theatres that reverberate with the sounds and sights of performers from all corners of the world. This is the embryo of the human mind enlarging in a pleasurable feast of the senses within a comfortable cocoon. It is the womb of enveloping joy at human creativity.

National Centre for Performing Arts, Tiananmen, Beijing. *(aasarchitecture.com)*

The French architect Paul Andreu had to solve a major design conundrum: the requirements of Beijing's planning laws meant that it could not exceed the height of 46 meters of the nearby Great Hall of the People, but its functional needs could not be crammed in a 46-meter space. The solution was to build 60% of the structure underground, as tall as ten stories, buoyed up by the abundant groundwater of an ancient river channel. To prevent the groundwater from seeping into the structure, a vast 'bucket' of subterranean concrete walls enclosed the foundation. A single 6,750-ton curved steel beam forms the world's largest dome, unsupported by a pillar. A "sound gate" technique ensured perfect acoustics for performers and audience (*National Centre*).

The marvels of design and problem solving recede into the distance as one listens, entranced, to the lush strings of the visiting Philadelphia Orchestra or the silken and passionate piano virtuosity of Beijing's home-grown geniuses, the irrepressible Lang Lang and Yuja Wang. This "egg" need never hatch, since it contains boundless riches within its lustrous shell.

Learning Activity (all ages): Blueprint for life
Design Your Own Wellness

Having explored the wonders of design masterpieces, we can apply some of their inspirations to the evolution of our own pathways. Each artist is propelled by their own vision, combining diverse elements and "thinking outside the box". In this activity, we can begin to conceive of designing "wellness", drawing upon multiple sources of physical and mental health. Examine the roles of diet, exercise, sport, friendship, empathy, beliefs, the needs of our "plastic, live-wired brain". Words as stimulants could pave the way for visual representations and musical compositions. Make lateral thinking our guide here – venturing outside the boundaries of our own communities and cultures, delving into the richness of the sciences, arts and humanities. Designing a "blueprint" for our lives conveys the excitement of an adventure that offers both clarity and the room for continual modification and improvisation. The structure remains incomplete, but extends much happiness and joy in its construction.

Cubism and Surrealism: Changing Angles and
Plunging Dreams

Although lateral thinking finds a place in every arena, artists are often at the forefront of disruptive and divergent conceptions that radically alter our awareness of reality. Blighted by the two most horrific conflicts in our history, the first half of the 20th century also generated art movements that foretold the birth of a new world. With Cubism, the human mind and eye was liberated from the prison of realistic representation, open to multiple perspectives and dissonant angles in transmitting the insights and emotions of the artist. Surrealism transported us into the realm of dreams and the subconscious, a realization that much of our lives were being sculpted below the surface of tangible experience.

Picasso (1907): *Les Demoiselles d'Avignon* (en.wikipedia.org)

Along with Fernand Leger, Pablo Picasso (1881-1973) is considered the founder of Cubism. In this work, the splintering of shapes enables us to view the human face and body from varied vantage points, a reminder of the incredible mobility of expression and emotion. The scarification on one face indicates Picasso's fascination with traditional African sculpture; in pushing the boundaries of modern art, he was transporting us back to its origins as well. With restless experimentation, Picasso continued to evolve different styles, making him one of the greats of all time. This art also signalled a cross-fertilization of ideas across cultures, the beckoning of a cosmopolitan and global outlook that gathered pace across the 20th and 21st centuries.

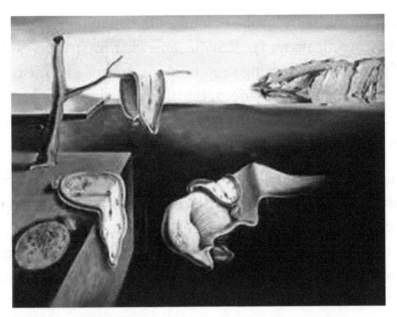

Salvador Dali (1931): *The Persistence of Memory* (blog.singulart.com)

Dali (1904-89) and other great Surrealist artists like Rene Magritte, Giorgio de Chirico, Max Ernst, Joan Miro and Leonora Carrington were fascinated by the insights of Sigmund Freud, the founder of modern psychoanalysis, and his explorations of the human psyche. The interpretation of dreams and their significance for the human personality became a richly ambiguous theme for the Surrealists. In this image, Dali's melting clocks could represent the ubiquity of time in our lives, but also its inconstant passage: in the dream state, time could appear to be frozen. Does the Africa-shaped clock in the left foreground symbolize the course of human history, or its degradation in the context of the parched landscape? The ants in the red dish are often seen as harbingers of death and decay, but for many bio-evolutionists they are the crucial ancestors of human traits such as planning and social collaboration. The central figure with the eyelash may be Dali's self-portrait, containing its own terrain of memories, distorted yet present. With his unique amalgam of technical brilliance and odd juxtaposition of objects, Dali ensured that the memory of his works would survive well beyond his time on earth.

Exploring Surrealist art involves a journey into manifold layers of interior worlds that we all share, yet remain somewhat mysterious and outside our daily awareness. Delving deep into our dreams and memories may emanate some painful sensations, but they can also be a liberating step toward emotional equilibrium and flourishing. The aesthetic flourish of art adds just the right colour and taste.

Surrealism has moved well beyond the boundaries of art into the world of consumer advertising and its surfeit of dream-like images, tapping into the subconscious mind in a form of "subliminal seduction"[75]. In that sense, Freud's penetrating insights and Dali's extravagant strokes (apart from his prosperous waxed moustache) have extended their reach into the deepest corners of the human brain.

Jazz and Raga: The Swing of Breathing Fire and Colourful Moods

Although arising in very different cultural contexts, the music of "jazz" and Indian "*ragas*" share the delights of improvisation and playful explorations of a dynamic range of sounds and emotions. Jazz stemmed primarily from African-American communities in the late 19th and early 20th centuries, carrying the imprint of West African roots and the historical experience in the American South; it probably derives from the slang "jasm", conveying energy and vitality. The African-based rhythmic technique of "swing" became the animating spirit of jazz, explained by the legendary Louis Armstrong: "if you don't feel it, you'll never know it" (*Jazz*). The *ragas*, foundational structures for Indian classical music, convey a similar intimacy with sentiment, emanating from the Sanskrit "*ranj*" or colouring with emotion (Massey 104). Jazz and *Raga* course through our veins, since sound or "*nada*" combines *na*, breath, and *da*, fire (92). This is a fire of unquenchable pleasure.

---

[75] A term used by psychologists to explain the persuasive power of images, which often bypass the rational prefrontal cortex in the brain and directly impact the memory and emotional centers.

Jazz branched into different styles as it interacted with regional and local musical cultures. New Orleans jazz relied primarily on blues and rag-time, with "collective polyphonic improvisation" (*Jazz*). Bebop and Cool Jazz in the 1940's introduced faster tempos and smoother sounds. Free jazz "explored playing without regular meter, beat and formal structures", and fusion forms such as jazz-rock and smooth jazz began to appear in the 1970s and '80s (*Jazz*). Latin and Afro-Cuban styles have added their flavour to this adaptable aesthetic, but preserved the key element of indi-viduality and performative freedom for the musician. Robert Christgau sums up its spacious appeal: "most of us would say that inventing mean-ing while letting loose is the essence and promise of jazz" (*Jazz*).

Listening Experience 1: The Very Best of Jazz
www.youtube.com/watch?v=SOGjGQteGMI&t=112s
April 11, 2020. Accessed: 2.5.2021

This album features many of the all-time Jazz greats: Louis Armstrong, Ella Fitzgerald, Miles Davis, Count Basie, Nat King Cole, Frank Sinatra, Nina Simone and Glenn Miller.

Listening Experience 2: Charlie Parker – Greatest Hits
https://www.youtube.com/watch?v=wTQMKRiYEZM
January 4, 2018. Accessed: 2.5.2021

Like Mozart, saxophonist and composer Charlie Parker, only lived 35 years (1920-55), but left his mark for ever with his innovative contribu-tions, particularly in *Bebop*.

Listening Experience 3: Relaxing Jazz Albums
Dave Stopera, BuzzFeed. January 16, 2021.

- Red Garland's Piano
- The Incredible Jazz Guitar of Wes Montgomery
- Dorothy Ashby: Afro-Harping

- Ahmad Jamal: Chamber Music of the New Jazz
- Antonio Carlos Jobin: Wave
- Kenny Burrell: Midnight Blue
- Ramsey Lewis: Mother Nature's Son
- John Coltrane and Johnny Hartman
- Johnny Smith: Moonlight in Vermont
- Stan Getz and Joao Gilberto: Getz/Gilberto
- Kenny Dorham: Quiet Kenny
- Milt Jackson and Wes Montgomery: Bags Meets Wes
- Bill Evans and Jim Hall: Undercurrent
- George Benson: Shape of Things to Come
- Coleman Hawkins and Ben Webster
- Wynton Kelly: Kelly Blue
- Chet Baker Quartet: No Problem
- Cannonball Adderley: Somethin' Else
- Gerry Mulligan meets Ben Webster
- Grant Green: Idle Moments

Indian classical music has evolved two distinct and fabulously rich traditions: the Carnatic (South Indian) and the Hindustani (North Indian). Both, though, derive from parent scales of the *raga*, radiating from a *vadi* keynote which gets elaborated, and illuminates each variation. Rather than progressing from this starting point, "Indian music revolves around it, probing it and examining it from every possible angle"[76] (Massey 108). Mood is as vital here as in jazz, and the performers "create it, explore it, and try to plumb its depths" (108). The masters induce a collective sigh of appreciation and wonder in the audience with a nuanced embellishment of *gamak,* grace notes. Partaking in an Indian classical concert makes for a covenant with collective euphoria.

---

[76] In that sense, Indian classical music seems to share some characteristics of Cubist art.

The moods and emotions evoked by the *raga* find unison with season and tempo. Blossoming spring and the earthy delight of monsoon rain discover complementary tones in the appropriate *raga*, which must also fulfil its congruent pulse at the relevant time of day and night. The music progresses from a meditative and calm "*alap*" to a moderately rhythmic "*jorh*" and "*jhala*", culminating in a fiery "*gat*" that explodes with the playful exchange between the soloist and percussionist, usually the drumming "*tabla*" in Hindustani and the "*mridangam*" in Carnatic (108-09). At its best, the "*jugalbandi*" partnership in the finale leaves the audience in spellbinding catharsis.

Listening Experience 4: MS Subbulakshmi – Evergreen Songs
https://www.youtube.com/watch?v=a76YER71adA
September 15, 2013. Accessed: 25.4.2021

The angelic voice of M.S. Subbulakshmi transmits the immortal traditions of Carnatic music, preserving the compositional brilliance and devotion of some of India's greatest minds. She is truly the nightingale of the heart and soul.

Listening Experience 5: Vilayat Khan (*sitar*) – Raga Yaman
www.youtube.com/watch?v=tGBKs7swowk&t=1425s
June 18, 2013. Accessed: 26.4.2021

Raga Yaman is suffused with the anticipation of a leisurely stroll and romantic conversation at the oncoming dusk and lengthening shadows. None conveys this better than Ustad Vilayat Khan, his *sitar* evoking the lyricism and tender nuances of the "*gayaki*"[77] style, emulating the golden voice of a celestial presence. This music leaves an eternal resonance and a longing for its continuation…into the dawn and beyond.

---

[77] Literally translates as "singing", a style that Vilayat Khan refined after learning vocal music with his mother.

Listening Experience 6: Shiv Kumar Sharma (*santoor*) and Zakir Hussain (*tabla*)

https://www.youtube.com/watch?v=Do69SJpAKoU
April 5, 2020. Accessed: 28.5.2021

The *santoor*, a dulcimer stringed instrument played with double mallets, probably originated in Persia and made its way to Kashmir along the historical Silk Route. The masterful strokes of Pandit Shiv Kumar Sharma glow with the paradisical beauty of Kashmir, the blend of sylvan valleys and pristine springs purified with mountain air, and the allure of its syncretic culture. The dazzling *tabla* of Ustad Zakir Hussain adds the fitting touch of exhilaration.

Listening Experience 7: Explore the World of *Ragas*

A good source are the **HCL** concerts and other sites on YouTube, just the tip of the iceberg of course for traditions that have been cultivated well over a millennium!

Carnatic (vocal)

- Semmangudi Srinivas Iyer
- Maharajapuram Santhanam
- Balamuralikrishna
- Madurai T.N. Seshagopalan
- Madurai Mani Iyer
- G.N. Balasubramaniam
- M.L. Vasantha Kumari
- D.K. Pattammal

Carnatic (instrumental)

- Mysore Doreswamy Iyengar (*veena*)
- Chitti Babu (*veena*)
- Ambalapuzha Brothers (*nadaswaram*)

- T.R. Mahalingam (flute)
- N. Ramani (flute)
- L. Subramaniam (violin)
- Lalgudi Jayaram (violin)
- Palghat Mani Iyer (*mridangam*)
- U. Srinivas (mandolin)

Hindustani (vocal)

- Bade Ghulam Ali Khan
- Bhimsen Joshi
- Dagar Brothers
- Parveen Sultana
- Gangubai Hangal
- Girija Devi
- Kumar Gandharva
- Kaushiki Chakraborty
- Singh Bandhu

Hindustani (instrumental)

- Ravi Shankar (*sitar*)
- Nikhil Banerjee (*sitar*)
- Rais Khan (*sitar)*
- Ali Akbar Khan (*sarod*)
- Amjad Ali Khan (*sarod*)
- Bismillah Khan (*shehnai*)
- Hariprasad Chaurasia (flute)
- Pannalal Ghosh (flute)
- V.G. Jog (violin)
- Allah Rakha (*tabla*)
- Zakir Hussain (*tabla*)

Photography: The Stillness of the Moment

"Taking pictures is savouring life intensely, every hundredth of a second."

Marc Riboud

"It is an illusion that photos are made with the camera… they are made with the eye, heart, and head."[78]

Henri Cartier-Bresson

Ever since the recorded image began to cast its spell in the 19th century, photography has extended its magic in ever widening circles of democratization; armed with the handphone camera today, photographs are truly "miniatures of reality than anyone can make or acquire" (Sontag 4). They seem the ideal intimate partners in an age of frenzied movement, travel to exotic destinations, virtual companionship, and consumerist celebration. As "evidence", images bolster individual and group self-promotion, ideologies, fashion trends, and identities in an imperial scope not attained by any other art form. Yet, they participate in an illusion of "permanence" in capturing the moment, for time has moved on: "precisely by slicing out this moment and freezing it, all photographs testify to time's relentless melt" (15). As we gaze at the faded visages of our grandparents and school friends, we are reminded that "to take a photo is to participate in another person's (or thing's) mortality, vulnerability, mutability" (15).

The "tragedy" of transience can also be its greatest asset and joy, for photography enables a passionate engagement with the world in its immense variation and fleeting grandeur. Paul Strand exclaimed that "the artist's world is limitless. It can be found anywhere far from where he lives or a few feet away. It is always on his doorstep". As a historian and

---

[78] All photographers' quotes sourced from: *Shot Kit – 96 most inspirational photography quotes* (updated April 13, 2021).

anthropologist, photography has become a passionate extension of my quest to meet and understand others who may not share my beliefs or worldviews, but contribute to the perpetual awe at our common humanity. I would agree heartily with Annie Leibovitz that "a thing that you see in my pictures is that I was not afraid to fall in love with these people". It is part of creating and nurturing "multiple selves", perhaps the most satisfying element in my personal journey.

With the geniuses of this art form, the "inner eye" of the camera melds with the mind's eye of the observer in conjuring the "perfect moment". The intuitive fusion may bear an urgent message, for the artist and the viewer are bonded by the image. Great landscape photographers like Ansel Adams conveyed the compelling need for Nature – "tamed, endangered, mortal" (Sontag 15) – to be protected from the reckless greed of humans, a higher imperative today. His portrayals managed to evade "time's relentless melt" and restored the abiding majesty of the primal force. He achieved a stillness that could only have arisen from a deep kinship with the subject, but recognized that art could not transcend all boundaries: "When words become unclear, I shall focus with photographs. When images become inadequate, I shall be content with silence." Silence in fact reigns in his vision.

Ansel Adams (1902-1984): *Yosemite National Park* (pinterest.com)

Meditation: The Stillness of the Mind

The attentional focus achieved by artists like Ansel Adams mirrors the quality realized in the practice of meditation.

Although often misrepresented as a spiritual convention or the search for a "peak" experience, meditation flows from an altered relationship to the mind and our personal narrative. Neuroscientist and philosopher, Sam Harris, suggests that much of our daily experience has an element of being lost in "thinking without knowing we are thinking", swayed by emotions and judgements about oneself or others that initiate a "war with our experience" (Harris). By disrupting this constant internal chatter and witnessing our thoughts and emotions in the role of an impersonal observer, we begin to disempower their destructive impact and move toward a greater comfort and centredness in the present moment; as Jon Kabat Zinn remarks, with the changed awareness you "get out of your own way" (Big Think).

The science backing the benefits of meditation is quite compelling. Research at Harvard University shows a lowering of blood pressure, improved immune systems, and shrinking in the brain area of stress at the seat of emotion (the amygdala) with short daily meditation (Big Think). The brain scans of Buddhist monks, who practice lifelong meditation for extended periods, reveal complete changes in the elec-tro-physiological responses. Their gamma waves, for example, remain at elevated levels, which for ordinary humans appear for just a half-second in the EEG spectrum[79]. When the monks meditate on compassion, the gamma waves jump to levels never seen before in science (Big Think). The levels of awareness and kindness, both to self and others, become a lasting trait. There is no vocabulary to capture that state of mind, but the practitioners reveal a spacious, open disposition, nourishing the needs

---

[79] The electroencephalogram test detects electrical activity in our "wired" brain.

of others. Losang Samten, director of the Chenrezig Tibetan Buddhist Centre in Philadelphia, discerns the seeds of this mental good quality in every person, awaiting patient sprouting and flourishing (Big Think).

Dan Harris of ABC News regards meditation as the "**next big public health revolution**", a "no-brainer" in the same class as balanced nutrition and physical exertion (Big Think). Although meditation schools and practices abound, it seems appropriate to honour a tradition rooted in the experience and teaching of the Great Liberator himself. *Vipassana*[80] preserves the Buddha's insistence on observing "reality as it is", what is happening right here, without trying to impose a story, or change it in any way (Goenka). There is no room for imagination, speculation, or dogma. The usual starting point is the observation of one's breath without any words, method or control, noticing the basic yet vital flow of life. Yuval Noah Harari, the brilliant Israeli historian, explains that with *Vipassana*, "you get to know the most ordinary daily natural experience – joy, anger, boredom – what you have to live with every day… (there is) no running away to fantasies, stories, fictions". It helps to confront "the deep source of so much of our personal and collective problems, the fantasies that we create and impose upon reality and becoming extremely upset when reality doesn't conform to our fantasy" (Harari). The regular practice of *Vipassana* has certainly conferred on Harari a laser-like clarity of mind and explanation, evident in his masterly history of the human species, *Sapiens*, and guidance for our contemporary concerns in *21 Lessons for the 21st century*.

The Buddha was always lucid and direct: "Let me tell you what I lost through meditation: sickness, anger, insecurity, depression, the burden of old age, the fear of death"[81].

---

[80] In Pali, the Buddha's language, it translates as "special seeing" or "insight". Vipassana meditation can be practiced for different durations.

[81] From the "*Dhammapada*" (the path of the universal law).

Sources/Citations

Arch Daily. Messner Mountain Museum Corones /Zaha Hadid Architects. https://www.archdaily.com. August 4, 2015.

Big Think. *"How Meditation can change your life and mind".* https://www.youtube.com/watch?v=jCJdl6Vs7wg August 7, 2020. Accessed: 6.5.2021

De Bono, Edward. 1970. *Lateral Thinking.* London, Penguin.

God's Architect: Antoni Gaudi's Glorious Vision (CBS News). https://www.youtube.com/watch?v=ZnNwpmdWm1w March 11, 2013. Accessed: 28.4.2021

Goenka, S.N. *"Shri S.N. Goenka on Vipassana Meditation".* https://www.youtube.com/watch?v=c9v8yHOM3r4 January 25, 2012. Accessed: 2.5.2021

Harari, Yuval Noah. *"Yuval Harari on Vipassana, Reality, Suffering, and Consciousness".* https://www.youtube.com/watch?v=i1_YhlXiuxE&t=4s May 15, 2018. Accessed: 4.5.2021

Harris, Sam. *"Sam Harris and Yuval Harari on Meditation".* https://www.youtube.com/watch?v=-pORbAOBan8 September 21, 2018. Accessed: 5.5.2021

Jazz. Wikipedia. https://en. wikipedia.org. Visited: 1.5.2021.

Massey, Reginald and Jamila. 1993. *The Music of India.* New Delhi, Abhinav Publications.

National Centre for the Performing Arts, Beijing. https://en. wikipedia.org. Visited: 27.4.2021.

Oxford Union. *"Dame Zaha Hadid – Full Q & A"*
https://www.youtube.com/watch?v=k0gLhcPOtdM
March 15, 2016. Accessed: 29.4.2021

Pink, Daniel H. 2005. *A Whole New Mind*. New York, Riverhead Books.

Sloane, Paul. 2017. *The Leader's Guide to Lateral Thinking Skills*. London, Kogan Page.

Sontag, Susan. 1977. *On Photography*. New York, Picador.

The Seventh Circle of Joy

We have now reached the zenith of energy flow, which dwarfs the other circles in its intensity and animation. The cranium vibrates with the sparks of a billion neurons in a constant dance of bonding and networking. Our pliable brain conducts a level of concentration and focus that harvests humanity's grandest achievements. This is the circle of synthesis, where diverse elements blend in a congenial and transformative synergy.

The movement that we nurtured in the earlier circles finds fruition in supreme sporting endeavour and achievement, a source of unbridled joy for performer and spectator. The moving image brings its own captivating combination of entertainment and insight, as film makers uncover myriad layers of our psyche. The cultivated and nimble mind finds space to explore some of our deepest inquiries, heightening the flame of innate curiosity kindled in the embryonic years. Divisions that arose in our quest earlier begin to melt as we realize the power of integration; a father and son guide us in an exciting symbiosis of perspectives from science and spirituality, a bridge that mirrors rich neural harmony.

With the collective brain of humanity as our faithful ally, we need renewed energy to confront some of the daunting challenges facing us today, from pandemics and climate change to preserving physical and mental health. The uncertainty created by these lurking perils spurs our attempts to find viable and durable solutions that will benefit succeeding generations. My most riveting and memorable moments as an educator arose in the lively dialogue and interaction with young minds in the "Theory of Knowledge", a course in critical thinking in the International Baccalaureate curriculum. We transcended the boundaries of subject areas in examining contemporary obstacles to human flourishing, as policy makers and leaders must do in tackling the urgent tasks ahead.

In all aspects of good thinking, individual effort and collaborative teamwork blend in a seamless and effective partnership. The leitmotifs of "connectedness" and "expansion" from the earlier circles return with added vigour, spanning the micro and macro spheres in integrated "mind maps" that guide a meaningful and pleasing existence . Tuning into and nourishing our brain forges the template for skilful living and aging, while social bonds add the patina of warm contentment. A respectful link with nature finds inspiration from artists, activists and the wisdom of indigenous cultures. We reach even higher, attempting to pierce the secrets of the universe or grasp its eternal pulse.

It is music, above all, that ennobles our existence. At the pinnacle emanates the symphony, weaving melody and rhythm, resounding with our breath, the senses, intuition, emotion, expression, and the inner vision. The seven circles coalesce here in an uplifting and zestful unity. The **cosmic mind** is our most majestic inheritance.

Sport: The Flow of Focused Excellence

There can be few sights in human experience more thrilling than witnessing an athlete at their performative prime: Michael Jordan pouching a three-pointer with effortless grace, Serena Williams completing a winner with potent precision, Tiger Woods bending the greens to his touches of genius, Sachin Tendulkar piercing the field with a poetic drive, Nadia Comaneci defying gravity on the bars and the floor, Pele confounding the goalkeeper with flawless curve. These are moments which leave us gasping in wonder and admiration, they propel us into a sphere of extraordinary delight. We are left breathless and speechless, having tasted moments of perfection which defy human limitation. We will never achieve these heights ourselves, but participation carries its own fulfilment.

Underlying these remarkable feats lies the reality of profound preparation and persistent effort. In a counterpoint to our increasingly distracted existence[82], distinction in sport builds upon an intense attentive ability, combining three elements of focus: the inner awareness of passion and talent, empathic capacity to coordinate with others, and a grasp of the "outer" systems of rules and strategies. Even in individual sports, "team work" reigns in tandem with coaches and mentors. Howard Gardner[83] views superior achievement as an alignment of "excellence, engagement, and ethics" (Goleman). Sportsmanship generates as much adulation as athletic brilliance. Roger Federer and Rafael Nadal, intense rivals on the tennis court, enhanced their reputation as two of the greatest players ever in maintaining respect for each other and honouring the opponent[84]. When sport blends our finest skills and instincts, it composes a beautiful melody in the heart and the mind, a "maximal neural harmony" (Goleman).

Viewing experience 1: The Last Dance (ESPN and Netflix series, 2020).

This series celebrates the 1998 season victory of the Chicago Bulls in the NBA[85] World Championships, helmed by Michael Jordan, arguably the greatest basketball player in history and a global superstar. Although Jordan created a brand of his own in multiple dimensions, he clarifies that "my game was my biggest endorsement...it did all the talking". Like all great champions, he helps us mirror the state of flow[86], and we can

---

[82] Nobel laureate Herbert Simon puts it succinctly: "a wealth of information creates poverty of attention".

[83] Professor of Cognition and Education at Harvard University, credited with emphasizing "multiple Intelligences", a paradigm shift away from the narrow focus on verbal and numerical abilities.

[84] Nadal proclaimed that "Federer is the best player in history, no other player has had such quality". Yet, Nadal himself has been virtually unbeatable on clay courts.

[85] National Basketball Association in the USA.

[86] Czech philosopher, Mihaly Csikszentmihalyi, defines flow as a " state of optimal experience", a fusion of intense concentration and skill, opening the door to ecstatic episodes.

marvel at the poetry in motion that he unleashed on the court. The element of catharsis in viewing MJ matches that of the grandest theatrical masterpiece.

English commentator, John Arlott, describes the presence and impact of Sir Garfield Sobers

The elegant yet combative game of cricket may have originated in the sylvan fields of England, but it soon found fertile germination throughout its colonial realm and the "Commonwealth" that emerged in the mid-20th century. The players of the Caribbean islands, collectively teamed as the West Indies, added a special flair and nimble poise to the sport, none more so than Sir Garfield (Garry) Sobers from Barbados, considered by most enthusiasts to be the greatest cricketer of all time. As an "all-rounder", his ability spanned all three aspects of the game: batting, bowling (at different speeds and variations), and fielding. Among the joys of my childhood and school years was listening to the "Test Match Special" radio broadcasts from the BBC, the commentators' keen eye and humour bringing the exploits alive to audiences at a distance of thousands of miles.

One of them, John Arlott, described the enchantment of Garry Sobers as a batsman: "Everything he did was marked by a natural grace, apparent at first sight. As he walked out to bat, six feet tall, lithe but with adequately wide shoulders, he moved with long strides which, even when he was hurrying, had an air of laziness, the hip joints rippling like those of a great cat. He was, it seems, born with basic orthodoxy in batting; the fundamental reason for his high scoring lay in the correctness of his defence. Once he was established (and he did not always settle in quickly), his sharp eye, early assessment, and inborn gift of timing, enabled him to play almost any stroke. Neither a back foot nor a front foot player, he was either as the ball and conditions demanded. When he stepped out and drove it was with a full flow of the bat and a complete follow through, in the classical manner. When he could not get to the pitch of the ball, he would go back, wait – as it sometimes seemed, impossibly long – until he identified it and then, at the slightest opportunity, with an explosive whip of the wrists, hit it with immense power. His quick reactions and natural ability linked with his attacking instinct made him a brilliant improviser of strokes. When he was on the kill it was all but impossible to bowl to him- and he was one of the most thrilling of all batsmen to watch" (Wisden). The hunting metaphor used by Arlott hints at the incredible appeal of cricket: moments of choreographed beauty coupled with intense competitiveness.

Viewing Experience 2: Fire in Babylon (2010, director Steve Riley; Amazon Prime)

This film celebrates the dominance of the West Indian cricket team for well over a decade in the 1970s and 1980s. There was much more than sport involved here; a form of historical retribution for the formerly enslaved and colonized people of the Caribbean. "Babylon", in the Rastafari vernacular of Jamaica, refers to the oppressive structure of colonial rule, and the "fire" was finally going to smother that legacy. The West Indies under captain Clive Lloyd went from being seen as an entertaining but beatable side to a formidable force, built on fearsome fast bowling and attacking batsmen. The comment in 1976 by the South African-turned English captain, Tony Greig[87], that he would make the West Indies "grovel", triggered a battering of the English batsmen and bowlers that set the trend for many years to come. For the Caribbean migrants to the UK, the heroics of the West Indies team became a source of pride and joy; cricket as a source of justice long denied. The "gentleman's game" could also become an arena of reckoning.

---

[87] This was at the height of the "apartheid" era of discrimination and separation of races in South Africa, and a prelude to the boycott of South African sports teams and commerce in the 1980s.

Viewing Experience 3: Perfection at every move

Nadia Comaneci (first perfect 10 – '76 Olympics):
https://www.youtube.com/watch?v=Yi_5xbd5xdE
June 26, 2012. Accessed: 14.5.2021
www.youtube.com/watch?v=Yl9QpC8_LiE&t=474s
April 28, 2013. Accessed: 14.5.2021

Simone Biles – Hardest Skills:
https://www.youtube.com/watch?v=sk5UiuNovU8
October 9, 2020. accessed: 15.5.2021

The 14-year-old Romanian, Nadia Comaneci, stunned and thrilled the world with the first "perfect 10" in gymnastics at the 1976 Montreal Olympics. Her thirty second routine on the uneven bars could not be recorded on the scoreboard, since there was no provision for a "10"! She went on to repeat the feat in other routines, swinging and balancing and pirouetting with practiced ease, leaving the spectators gasping with wonder at each turn. Today, we are awestruck by the amazing dexterity of the American gymnast, Simone Biles, who appears to defy the laws of physics. If sport is a play of the angels, Nadia Comaneci and Simone Biles gift us glimpses of celestial dazzle.

Film: Journeys of the Soul

"Film is like music – the measure of our breath".

Ingmar Bergman

The moving picture has held us in thrall since its invention over a century ago. The cave-like ambience of the film theatre heightens the sense of fantasy and intimacy as the visual feast enters directly into our subconscious realm. Over the years, film has become an intricate choreography of image, sound, setting, casting, costume and technology; at its heart, though, remains the visceral experience of the viewer. Great directors like Chaplin and Welles left their mark on early filmmaking, but arguably the golden age of cinema spanned from the 1960's to 1980's – the era of the profound artistry of Ingmar Bergman in Sweden, Alfred Hitchcock and Stanley Kubrick in the UK and USA, Akira Kurosawa in Japan, Satyajit Ray in India, Michelangelo Antonioni, Federico Fellini and Pier Paolo Pasolini in Italy, Francois Truffaut, Robert Bresson and Jean-Luc Godard in France, Rainer Fassbinder and Werner Herzog in Germany, Andrei Tarkovsky in Russia, Luis Bunuel in Spain/Mexico. Bergman said that "many of my films are about journeys, about people going from one place to another" (Bjorkman 147). The universality of this theme strikes a deep nerve, and the greats of cinema have the ability to transform the journey for us all.

Viewing Experience 4: *Wild Strawberries* **(1957, director Ingmar Bergman).**
https://www.youtube.com/watch?v=IZhYtsGJz78
January 17, 2021. Accessed: 5.5.2021.

At 78, Professor Isak Borg has a dream of a clock with no hands, and a hearse which crashes into a lamp post, spilling the coffin with his body onto the street. It is a reckoning with mortality that all humans must confront. The actor who played Borg, Viktor Sjostrom, was himself a distinguished director from whom Bergman learned "his incorruptible demand for truth, his incorruptible observation of reality" (Bjorkman 136). Bergman's film is a searing examination of the layers of reality that construct individual personality and character, peeled back in screen time. The Borg family seems to transmit an emotional frigidity, stretching from Isak's mother to his son, Evald, who tells him that "I was an unwanted child in a hellish marriage…this life sickens me". Evald's wife, Marianne, is equally unsparing of Isak, calling him "selfish and ruthless, hidden behind a charming exterior". Evald seems to be growing as lonely and cold as his father. Yet, on his way to be honoured for his services as a medical officer, Isak is reminded by the townspeople of his kindness, "which can never be paid back". Three youngsters, who take a ride with Isak, celebrate his achievement with flowers and serenade him, singing that "he must know everything about life".

Isak's greatest comfort and solace is to return to his childhood, and he makes a stop at the place where he spent the summer for twenty years with the family: "If I have been worried or sad during the day, it often calms me to recall childhood memories". He recalls his love for his cousin Sara, who married the "more bold and exciting" Sigfrid, and of the merry picnics in the spot where wild strawberries grew. For Bergman, the starting point of *Wild Strawberries* was the idea, "supposing I make a film of someone coming along, perfectly realistically, and suddenly opening a door and walking into his childhood? And then opening another door and walking out into reality again?" (133).

Nostalgia touches a chord in each of us, as well as the realization of the complexities of our conditioning. We cannot condemn Isak for his failings, and the softening of Marianne towards him by the end of the film may open another door of redemption. Bergman's own journey offers a lesson in the expansion of possibility: "My basic view of things is – not to have any basic view of things. From having been exceedingly dogmatic, my views on life have gradually dissolved. They don't exist any longer" (17).

Viewing Experience 5: Fellini Satyricon (1969, director Federico Fellini).

https://www.youtube.com/watch?v=kkaKV7v2oEU
April 28, 2017. Accessed: 17.5.2021

"Abundance has liberated us, but not fulfilled us".

Daniel H. Pink

In *Satyricon,* Fellini takes us back to imperial Rome, with a collection of stories written by Petronius, an adviser to Emperor Nero. The plot centres on two adolescent Romans, Encolpio and Ascilto, who are kidnapped by a pirate and enslaved upon a boat. Once freed, they launch upon a series of voluptuous adventures, which end with Encolpio boarding a ship to Africa and turning into a fresco, in keeping with the episodic nature of the film. This is a luscious and sensual journey into a surrealist world, filled with the most extraordinary characters that Fellini managed to discover in present-day Rome and the phenomenal sets created by Danilo Donati. However, similar to Fellini's earlier classic, *La Dolce Vita, Satyricon* is a critique of contemporary society and its materialistic obsessions: "for Fellini, the lives of the ancients are just as dissipated and filled with empty pursuits as those of the people who frequent via Veneto (Rome's premier shopping and fashion avenue)… *Satyricon's* bored young characters, clinging desperately to their adolescence…go about their pleasures mechanically, resigned to their perversions" (Wiegand 116).

Fellini's extraordinary vision carries deep resonance in our time; a prescient warning that unprecedented material abundance often comes at the cost of alienation, both from others, and from the self.

Viewing Experience 6: *Nomadland* (2020, director Chloe Zhao).

The winner of the Oscar for best film in 2020 marked only the second time that a woman director has won the award, and the first of Asian ancestry. The trend toward greater inclusion and diversity in the Oscars is certainly a welcome, if belated, recognition of the contribution of multiple voices in the global reach and fascination of Hollywood. The best film award in 1919 to the Korean director, Bong Joon-ho's "*Parasite*" marked the embrace of talent from a tiny but adventurously creative corner of the world.

In a year when we were forced to shelter at home by an invisible menace and curb our instincts for outdoor and communal pursuits, there was something compelling about *Nomadland*, a film that celebrates an individual on the move, a life on the road. Fern (played brilliantly by Frances McDormand, who won the Oscar for best actress) becomes a guide into the rich world of nomadic living. Director Chloe Zhao says she discovered two kinds of nomads: the "true nomads", who always want to hit the road and belong there, and others who use the road as a means to an end, such as economic recovery. She views the film not as a social commentary, preferring the audience to make its own judgement: "we're not here to teach, but to communicate something" (TIFF). The self-reliance and wisdom of Fern find a perfect backdrop in the exquisitely expansive American landscape. Having grown up in cities, deprived of a close bonding with nature, Chloe realized during the filming how much she needed it: "I think nature humbles you, and puts you in perspective all the time" (TIFF). The Chinese Confucian heritage of Chloe Zhao also surfaces in her respectful treatment of elders and the mature faces in *Nomadland*; they are likened to the Saguaro cactus, the value and treasure of having been there for a long time. Frances McDormand appreciates that "Chloe has a real connection to the cycle of human life; the exploration of seniors and seasoned people is part of that landscape too" (TIFF).

Fern's journey in *Nomadland* finds the pulse of the nomad and the wanderer in us all.

Philosophy: the wisdom of integration

"Philosophy is an integral metamorphosis in one's way of living".

Jean-Francois Revel

Ever since emerging as *homo sapiens* and overcoming the early obstacles to survival, humans have privileged thinking as a reliable partner in our capacity to construct ways of living that enrich our presence on earth.

Whether out of necessity in confronting danger, or in exuberant celebration of the bounty presented by nature and our own creations, the human brain and our collaborative instincts have guided us through peril and triumph. Over time, the metacognitive aptitude developed an ability to look well beyond tangible matter, to probe the multiple layers of reality, and to turn the spotlight on our own thought. All flourishing civilizations accorded the crowning glory to philosophy, the domain of thought that could investigate the disparate strands of existence and unite them into a path that pointed toward deep understanding and flourishing. Philosophy always thrived on the inquiring quest and dialogue, enhancing our instincts of curiosity and buoyant chatter.

Reading Experience 1: The Monk and the Philosopher

The Monk and the Philosopher is an absorbing conversation between a father and son: Jean-Francois Revel, a French philosopher and humanist, and his son Matthieu Ricard, who started a career in molecular biology before becoming a Tibetan Buddhist monk, living in India and Nepal. Their ideas open up the possibility of a rich interaction between the Western and Eastern traditions of rationality and spirituality, a meaningful synthesis that we could adopt in the face of our own existential dilemmas. One of the intriguing puzzles concerns the rapid development of **artificial intelligence**, and the fears that it may displace jobs and pose a threat to our autonomy with its surveillance algorithms. Revel states the "materialist monist" view that has held sway in Western scientific thought for the last three hundred years: "Man is a material being, part of the biological sphere like other forms of life. The true distinction is between matter and life. Life, moreover, is derived chemically from matter. Consciousness arises from a set of neuro-cerebral factors, particularly language, evolution's latest development" (Revel, Ricard 56). Could artificial intelligence, powered by supercomputing ability, emerge as a form of consciousness in itself and challenge humanity as its core? Ricard makes a strong defence of what makes us truly "human": "It's more revealing to look at what artificial intelligence is **not** capable of doing. It can 'play' but knows nothing of the spirit of playfulness. It can calculate the future but could never worry about it; it can record the past but could never feel joy or sadness about it. It doesn't know how to laugh or cry, be sensitive to beauty or ugliness, or feel friendship or compassion" (57).

Could we reconcile the rational, scientific part of our thought patterns with the quest for faith and spiritual truths? For Revel, "what characterizes rational thought is that all the evidence can be communicated to anyone, and they can even be obliged to admit its validity – even those who haven't themselves observed the experiment being carried out" (77-78); the replicability and verification of experiments contributes to their certainty. Ricard asserts that "the certainty arising from a life of contemplative practice, or a life lived with a spiritual teacher, is just as powerful as that arising from the demonstration of a theorem. As for its experimental verification, the only difference is that it's usually inner, which removes none of its authenticity. Its outer aspects – goodness, tolerance, compassion, wisdom – are only 'signs' of inner realization" (78). With our dynamic and spacious brain, it seems perfectly plausible to explore both practices and to gain immense delight from them.

We could also benefit from different understandings of the role of individualism and the self. Revel points out that Western civilization places much importance on the strong personality. Exceptional periods in history such as the Italian Renaissance were shaped by cultivated princes like Federico d'Urbino and the Medicis as well as artist-scientists like Leonardo da Vinci: "we also admire great philosophers, artists, and writers, but not nearly as much as men of action, men who transformed the world, organizers who reformed societies" (152). Ricard counters that "it's important not to confuse strong individuality and strength of mind. The great teachers I've been able to meet ...had very impressive personalities, and they radiated a sort of natural strength that everyone who met them could perceive. But the big difference was that you couldn't find the slightest trace of ego in them…their strength of mind came from knowledge, serenity, and inner freedom that were outwardly manifested as an unshakable certainty" (153). The creative originality and inventiveness of Western scientists and artists can be tempered with the Buddhist belief in our ability to dissolve "pride, vanity, obsession, touchiness, and acrimony" (156).

History and "progress" can carry different connotations. Revel claims that "the whole of Western civilization is oriented toward history. It believes in historical evolution and in the productivity of time…the quality on which (it) sets the highest price is (that) of novelty" (306). The premium on "new ideas" in science and innovation in the arts, technology and politics are all manifestations of this imperative. Ricard reminds us, though, that "if you're always looking for novelty, you're often depriving yourself of the most essential truths…(rather) the novelty that's always 'new' is the freshness of the present moment, of nowness, of clear awareness that's not reliving any past or imagining any future"(307).

With the thriving of global exchange in our time, "spiritual and temporal can be combined in an intelligent and constructive way…The West has produced antibiotics that save human lives, and Tibet has spent its time giving meaning to existence" (161). We have the makings of a pleasing symphony here.

Reading Experience 2: Einstein and Buddha – Quantum Realities

For Wes Nisker, the dialogue of scientific and spiritual traditions heralds "the full-brain approach", modelled on the corpus callosum, "connecting the two hemispheres (of the brain) and revealing an astonishing agreement about the laws of nature and the structure of deep reality" (in McFarlane viii). The insights of Einstein on relativity, Heisenberg's "uncertainty principle", and quantum physics have validated Buddhist notions of impermanence: "while the scientist has discovered that everything is in constant flux by examining the external world, the meditator will discover this same truth inside his or her mind and body" (ix). Their complementary quest underlines the gripping dialectic of faith and doubt, of logic and intuition: "although the scientist must be willing to doubt every physical hypothesis, the practice of science calls for fundamental faith that reality is rationally comprehensible. The spiritual seeker, too, must begin with faith that the ultimate truth can be known, but will never know that truth without a radical doubt of all human forms of knowledge" (McFarlane xv).

Despite the vast advances through time in scientific and spiritual knowledge, and in their applications and practices, what is most commendable is the **humility** at the heart of both enterprises. Einstein admitted that "all our science, measured against reality, is primitive and childlike"; Chinese sage Chuang Tzu realized that to "calculate what man knows... cannot compare to what he does not know" (56). Human limitation imposes its own constraints. German physicist Max Planck conceded that "this world faces us with the impossibility of knowing it directly....it is a world whose nature cannot be comprehended by our human powers of mental conception"; similarly the Indian thinker, Shankara, averred that "Brahman (the ultimate, highest reality) is outside the range of any mental conception" (57).

Even the atom, once considered the smallest indivisible element in matter, is now seen to have no fixed essence, as physics takes us into the realm of sub-atomic matter and "quanta". Werner Heisenberg, German physicist, explains that " the atoms or the elementary particles...form a world of potentialities or possibilities rather than one of things or facts". Zen scholar D.T. Suzuki sees parallels with the Buddhist idea of Emptiness, where "there is no time, no space, no becoming, no-thing-ness; it is what makes all things possible; it is a zero full of infinite possibilities, it is a void of inexhaustible contents" (110). Stanford neuro-scientist David Eagleman is an eager proponent of "**possibilianism**", an open-minded outlook that coheres with the expansive qualities of the brain (Eagleman).

The realization of our limited grasp of reality becomes the catalyst for ever more daring inquiries into the nature of physical and mental phenomena. Could we discover a unifying element in our universe, even as we recognize our insignificance in the "multiverse"[88]? Theoretical physicists like Michio Kaku, professor at City College of New York, hold out the tantalizing possibility that "the subatomic particles that we see in nature are nothing but musical notes on a tiny vibrating string[89]", and the universe could be "a symphony of vibrating strings" (Kaku). The "**string theory**" posits an eleven-dimensional universe that brings together gravity, electromagnetism, strong and weak nuclear forces. The concept of vibrating strings is particularly pleasing, promising the unison of our most beautiful art form and the investigative mind. We could be on the cusp of celebrating the **cosmic music** that binds all life.

Critical thinking in an age of information overload

> "A gentleman can see a question from all sides without bias. A small man is biased and can only see a question from one side."
>
> Confucius

While philosophy and the sciences enlighten our minds in diverse dimensions, human societies today face an imminent threat in coping with a deluge of information unleashed by the explosion of sources on the internet and social media. These seem to encourage some of the most negative human tendencies, with misinformation, "fake news" and outright falsehoods swirling around us; the Covid pandemic tended to magnify the trend. We can observe the "balkanization" of news sources as people

---

[88] Scientists are convinced of the existence of several universes, and ours may have formed after a collision or fission (breaking away) from another, which may explain the "Big Bang" or genesis of life (*The Universe*).

[89] Similar to the insight from Indian philosophy that life originated in a primal vibration.

cope with the overload by retreating into "silos" and "echo chambers" that confirm their own assumptions, and the inability to acknowledge or debate perspectives that differ from their own. Among the casualties of this narrowing appears to be evidence-based reasoning, with often devastating consequences for countries and institutions[90].

To confront this immediate and real challenge, the case for **critical thinking** to be introduced in schools[91] and reinforced in adult learning could not be more urgent. Employers have identified critical thinking, comprising manifold elements, as the primary competency for 21st century learning and application in the workplace and society (WEF). This flows from the recognition that reasoned analysis, a consideration of multiple options, thinking laterally, collaborative inputs, and perceptive reflection construct the ideal conduits in an era demanding innovation, adaptability, resilience, effective teamwork, and global frameworks. The root for "critical" derives from "criteria", implying disciplined and evidence-based thinking, our best defence against false claims and assertions of a "post-truth" age[92].

Critical thinking, honed at school, becomes an essential partner in lifelong practice. Coupled with creative inputs and problem solving imperatives, we adopt it as the indispensable ally in tackling the demanding perils of climate change, global pandemics, energy depletion, and environmental destruction, as much as social quandaries of discrimination, inequality, and exclusion. Collaboration and open-minded inquiry underlie the

---

[90] An example would be the response to Covid-19 in countries like Brazil, India, and the US, whose leaders ignored the scientific evidence on the virus, causing lack of preparedness and tragically high mortality.

[91] The I.B. (International Baccalaureate) curriculum, adopted by many schools today, includes a core element of critical thinking in the Theory of Knowledge course, which must be completed by each student.

[92] The Oxford dictionary definition implies that in a "post-truth" society, objective facts are less influential in shaping public opinion than appeals to emotion and personal belief.

elation in learning from others, the springboard of a sophisticated and discerning worldview and a dynamic mental map. Above all, critical thinking demands turning the spotlight on ourselves. Only persistent engagement with diverse perspectives and constant reflection on one's own thought and action can become the antidote to the extensive and deep-seated biases – of birth, race, gender, ethnicity, nationality, religion, social class, education, politics – the poisoned and piercing arrows that have resulted in human conflict and destructive attitudes through the ages.

Like all good thinking, though, there is room here for ambiguity and uncertainty, a humbling acceptance of the "graciousness of not knowing…(of being) present in the unfolding mystery of life" (Kornfield).

Learning Activity: SARS and Covid-19 through multiple lenses

"If our small minds, for some convenience, divide this universe into parts – physics, biology, geology, astronomy, psychology and so on – remember that nature does not know it! So let us put it all back together".

Richard P. Feynman (physicist)

Critical thinking, in its exploration of divergent perspectives, begins to remove the boundaries between subject areas and encourage trans-disciplinary inquiries that develop a more holistic mindset. When confronted with a crisis like the global pandemic, this approach becomes essential in carving an adequate response. During the SARS[93] pandemic in 2003, a group of six high school students from different parts of the world collaborated online to design and upload an engaging educational

---

[93] "Severe acute respiratory syndrome", a corona virus with similarities to Covid-19. It was largely confined to East Asia.

website, which included research findings about SARS, interviews with experts, and informative text[94]. "The student team was confronted with an immense amount of content knowledge, including the biology of the SARS virus, the medical reports on the virus's effects on the body, the most effective ways to prevent and treat the disease, the mathematical and epidemiological data on the spread of the disease, and the social and governmental responses to monitoring and controlling the outbreak" (Trilling and Fadel 51). The project fused critical thinking and problem solving in an effective manner: "The team's challenge was to use their critical thinking skills – the ability to analyse, interpret, evaluate, summarize, and synthesize all (the) information – and apply the results to solve an urgent problem: getting other students to overcome their fears by learning more about the disease and about ways to protect themselves from the viral outbreak" (51). This was a commendable effort to replace fear, panic, and rumour with credible and well-founded information.

Middle and high school students can adopt a similar trans-disciplinary and teamwork approach in studying the impact of Covid-19:

- Mathematical models and statistics to chart and predict the spread and progression of the disease in different parts of the world, the number of infections and mortality rates.
- Scientific data from biology, epidemiology, and immunology on the nature of the virus, the probable causes and the effective steps to control and overcome the pandemic.
- Information from public health officials, pharmacology and laboratories on medical treatments and development of effective vaccines.
- The political response by leaders and governments in containing the virus.

---

[94] The SARS project, developed as part of a global competition called *ThinkQuest*.

- The economic and technological effects, short and long term, of policy measures like "lockdowns" and changes in work patterns.
- The psychological impact on mental health and relationships for different age groups.
- A historical view in comparing Covid-19 with earlier global pandemics like the Plague (Black Death) and the "Spanish flu" in 1918-1920.
- The creative response of artists, in multiple genres, including innovative works by artists like *"Beeple"*[95].
- A philosophical consideration of the ethical consequences of the pandemic, especially the differential impact on social groups and countries.

As with the SARS project, the goal here is to develop a well-informed and evidence-based response among students, who will soon take their place as the citizenry in their respective nations.

The holistic picture and the emphasis on global cooperation and action will also hopefully prepare us more effectively for future crises or, even better, prevent them altogether. This takes on greater urgency as we face a threat to the planet itself.

Conversation: Can a story save the planet? (Hammer Museum, Los Angeles. October 20, 2020).

Although a global pandemic like Covid-19 has directly and fiercely slammed our defences and lifestyles, scientific evidence and a series of catastrophic natural disasters portend a looming peril with potentially even more dire consequences for our existence on the planet. Climate change and its impact on communities are now an undeniable reality,

---

[95] Digital artist, Mike Winkelmann, or "Beeple" sold his work called *"Everydays: The First 5000 days"* for 69 million dollars in NFT or "non-fungible tokens", which is a digital asset, at a Christie's auction in March 2021.

but as an ongoing and relatively gradual process, it has not received adequate attention from a media consumed with daily events or even from fiction writers. Indian novelist Amitav Ghosh, author of "*The Great Derangement: Climate Change and the Unthinkable*" calls it an "evasion" and a "heightened delusion" to continue with this ignorance. In a conversation with Scott Burns, who wrote the screenplay for the prescient film "*Contagion*", and Elizabeth Kolbert, a journalist and author of "*The Sixth Extinction*", Ghosh discussed the possibilities of redressing this anomaly.

In our Anthropocene[96] era, we may have to return to our earliest art form to inform and persuade people of the palpable dangers of climate change. Burns avers that "the onus is on **story tellers** to spread the science". Kolbert sees the obstacles since this is not a discrete event, and in narratives requiring characters and closure, there is "no distinct story arc"; climate change requires a long-term perspective, whose outcomes are not easily predictable. Ghosh is inspired by the **Native American tradition**, which "found ways of incorporating non-human presences and agencies" in their stories and practices; it was "part of their imagining and life"[97]. Moving away from human-centred narratives, we could begin to include natural forces like "Hurricane Sandy" and "Arctic Ice Flows" as characters with their own story[98]. At a human level, though, we see the visceral and tangible effects on farmers, fishermen, and coastal city dwellers, vividly portrayed in "*Gun Island*" by Ghosh.

---

[96] A term used by some scientists to describe the current period in the earth's evolution, dating from the Industrial Revolution in the late 18th century CE and marked by an increasingly harmful impact on the environment due to human action, exemplified by the ever expanding "carbon footprint" of human activity, destruction of natural habitats, and endangering or extinction of animal and plant species.

[97] For an example of the continuation of this Native American sensibility, refer to Gail Tremblay's poem, "*Indian Singing in 20th century America*" on pages 146-147.

[98] See page 64 for a learning activity geared to young children, which introduces story telling using natural landscapes as characters.

Burns points out that pandemics also have deep links with climate, given our destructive relations with nature and the incursions into wild places, which breed new disease vectors[99]. Ghosh identifies "the mistaken idea of endless progress" as one of the contributing causes to our extending "footprint", riding roughshod over other forms of life. However, there are signs of optimism as well. The heroes include those committed to regenerative agriculture and the protection of endangered species. The teenage climate activist Greta Thunberg has touched a chord among school students and policy makers alike. Global leadership and cooperation led to the Paris Accord on the United Nations Framework on Climate Change in 2015[100]. When faced with the "radical uncertainty" about the future of our planet, a combination of political will and individual action gives us hope of constructing a story with a pleasing outcome for our future generations.

Joyful Aging: Transformational Connectedness

"If every day is an awakening, you will never grow old. You will just keep growing".

Gail Sheehy, author

A common belief in many societies portrays aging as a process of mental deterioration and creeping senility, and elders as a burden on their families and societies. There is increasing evidence that this is a flawed story that needs to be reviewed and rewritten. Gail Sheehy, author of the celebrated *"Passages: Predictable Crises of Adult Life"* (1976), paints a very different picture. She attests that "looking back over the many stages and passages I have studied and experienced, I can personally vouch

---

[99] An example is the extension of mosquito zones due to rising global temperatures.

[100] After a hiatus of four years, the USA reinstated its commitment to the Paris agreement with the election of President Joe Biden.

for one finding in all my studies: the most satisfying stages are those in our second adulthood. Simply, **older is better**. And never more so than today" (*Times*). We can credit the incredible advances in modern medicine which have doubled average lifespans in the last century, opening up possibilities for multiple careers, as well as the growing prosperity in many societies and the rapid diffusion of the internet, enabling lifelong learning. In some cultures, the veneration of elders continues to support a sense of worth and dignity into the culminating years of the life cycle[101].

Neuroscience offers accurate and nuanced confirmation of Sheehy's findings. Prof. Thad Polk of the University of Michigan refers to studies of aging in the brain that examine two kinds of processing – **fluid** (which deals with recognition of patterns and logical reasoning, and doesn't depend on what you know) and **crystallized** (which looks at knowledge and acquired skills). Aging is seen to have a greater impact on fluid processing, while older people do better on crystallized, indicating that our procedural memory for skills and habits remains intact. This also implies an improvement in emotional processing and in resolving interpersonal conflict, generating greater life satisfaction at the age of 65 than at 20. As Polk affirms, our brains don't take aging lying down and many aspects of our mental ability remain; in fact, they reorganize themselves to process information more efficiently. If we keep the brain active and explore new areas of interest, we could rewrite aging as a narrative of **transformation** rather than of deterioration (Polk).

However, we need to be mindful of the rising incidence of cognitive decline and dementia, most notably Alzheimer's disease, in aging populations worldwide. With the prospect of living three or more decades after retirement, a shrinking of horizons and social engagement, as well as lifestyle factors, emerge as realities which show up in ravaged tissues and damaged structures in brain scans. Dr. Daniel Amen, the American

---

[101] This is particularly the case in Asian and African cultures.

psychiatrist and brain disorder specialist, has identified multiple risk factors in scanning over 100,000 brains. Among them, "**diabesity**", a combination of high blood sugar and obesity, ranks as a disaster for brain function; the highly processed, high glycemic, pesticide-sprayed and low fibre diet promoted by the modern food industry contributes to an unhealthy population and what Amen terms "the biggest brain drain in American history" (Amen). Mental health is equally vital, since ANT's (automatic negative thoughts) can begin to ravage the mind and affect physical and cognitive wellbeing.

The positive aspect of Amen's scans is that "you can literally change people's brains, and when you do…you change their life" (Amen). We have already observed the benefits of healthy diets, physical exertion, and diaphragmatic breathing upon brain function in earlier chapters. Neuroscience and humanities concur on the importance of maintaining and widening community networks. A 75-year study at Harvard University showed conclusively that those with better social connectedness live longer (*7 Habits*). Investing in other people and in novel pursuits reduces the possibility of cognitive defects since one is "building new bridges" in the aging process.

Eagleman calls this "directed plasticity", since the brain is "a dynamic living electric fabric, constantly reconfiguring its own circuitry" (*Neuroplasticity*). With continued advancements in medical and genetic interventions, Dr. David Sinclair at Harvard foresees a further extension of the human lifespan and of "living longer in a youthful stage" (Sinclair).

Adopting our brain and others (humans and nature) as best friends, we may indeed be entering an era of a flourishing and deeply pleasing second adulthood. We may take inspiration from Captain Sir Tom Moore, who walked a hundred laps of his garden at age 99 to raise funds for the British National Health Service charities as it battled the Covid wave. He will always be remembered for telling us that "Tomorrow will be a good day".

Learning Activity: Mental Maps and Mind Metaphors (for older students and adults)

In the earlier circles, we saw the emergence and development of "mental maps" as the guideposts in sculpting our motivation, action, and world-view. In the seventh circle, these maps exude the vitality of integration, drawing upon the power of metaphor to span diverse areas of experience. As Prof. Anna Schaffner of the University of Kent indicates, "the metaphors we live by shape our existence…this is particularly true of the metaphors we conjure to describe our inner lives" (Schaffner). She points out that the dominant "mind-metaphors" today are shaped by technology (the "mind-as-computer") and the worlds of finance and business, which privilege "self-optimisation", reducing us to mechanistic entities and casting us as individualized competitors in a race with few "winners".

These notions contrast markedly with "the much older ideas of self-cultivation and *Bildung*: a life-long process of socio-psychological formation, learning and inner development" (Schaffner). The approach in "Joy Quotient" adopts a similar perspective, learning from the wisdom traditions of earlier cultures and from the imagery of nature, encouraging us to "nurture our virtues patiently, as we would nurture seedlings in a garden, so that we might grow and blossom" (Schaffner).

The mental maps that emerge from this careful and patient tending echo the learning activities and outlook at the core of this book, " understood as a work in progress, a process rather than a fixed entity, as dynamic rather than static"; moreover, they strive for a connectedness with ever widening circles of interaction, so that our mind-metaphors may begin to "(compare) us to bees, for example, to threads in a multi-layered fabric; or to tiny, multicoloured mosaic stones, each unique and distinctive, but together forming a beautiful work of art " (Schaffner). The natural and artistic worlds instil a powerful integrative imagination in our evolving voyage.

In this activity, you could select metaphors that best describe your motivation, values, experiences, and aspirations. Sharing these with classmates or a community of friends may design a colourful and delightful mosaic, composing life as an artwork worthy of its creators.

Cosmic Light: The Radiance of Vincent Van Gogh

"Sometimes I long so much to do landscape, and in all of nature, in trees for instance, I see expression and a soul".

Vincent Van Gogh

Van Gogh (1853-90) lived a short and tormented life, yet bestowed upon us a treasure of art works that pulsate with extraordinary vitality, reaching from deep within the human heart to realms at the edges of our consciousness. He painted *The Starry Night* in 1889 from the room of the mental asylum at Saint-Remy-de Provence.

Source: *www.vincentvangogh.org/starry-night.jsp* (accessed 25.5.2021).

Van Gogh painted *The Starry Night* in a period of intense personal suffering, but the painting seemed to transcend the trauma with an expressive vision that intrigues scientists and mathematicians today. Observing through the Hubble Space Telescope in 2004, scientists saw the eddies of a distant cloud of dust and gas around a star, which reminded them of the depiction in *The Starry Night* (St. Clair). This prompted a study of Van Gogh's luminance, the intensity of light in the colours on his canvas, which discovered a "distinct pattern of turbulent fluid structures" conforming to the Russian mathematician Andrey Kolmogorov's equations on turbulent flow. The digitization of the painting and the measurement of brightness variation between any two pixels confirmed that "the curves measured for pixel separations behave remarkably similar to fluid turbulence" (St. Clair).

Incredibly, Van Gogh was "able to perceive and represent one of the most supremely difficult concepts of nature, to unite his unique mind's eye with the deepest mysteries of movement, fluid and light" (St. Clair). A man with sorrow and illness had reached out to nature and beyond in a transcendent vision. "Everything here is brewed in a huge cosmic fusion…he was searching for the essence of the landscape, its very being – a way of registering its symbolic power, its vitality, its flux and constancy, all in one" (*Vincent*).

The tall cypress tree in the painting seems to reach from earthly existence to the redemption of the heavens above. A great artist unites us with the universe and its ceaseless flow.

Cosmic tones: the symphonic rapport of Beethoven and Brahms

Like Van Gogh, Beethoven (1770-1827) endured agony for a considerable period of his life, in his case after the onset of deafness at the age of 30. His indomitable will and commitment to the creative urge ensured a legacy of magnificent masterpieces that continue to enthral and enlighten millions today. The great painter linked us to the universe, and Beethoven bonded humanity and the heavens in an alluring vision of unity and fellowship. In his ninth symphony, he adopted Friedrich Schiller's poem *"An de Freude"* (Ode to Joy) for the rousing final movement[102], fusing instrument and voice in a resonating cry for universal peace and friendship:

Ode to Joy (extract)

Joy! A spark of fire from heaven,
Your magic power binds together,
What we by custom wrench apart,
All men will emerge as brothers,
Where you rest your gentle wings.

All creation drinks with pleasure,
Drinks at Mother Nature's breast;
All the just, and all the evil,
Follow down her rosy path.
Kisses she bestowed, and grape wine,
Friendship true, proved e'en in death;
Every worm knows nature's pleasure,
Every cherub meets his God.

Be embraced, all you millions,
Share this kiss with all the world!
Way above the stars, brothers,
There must live a loving father.
Do you kneel down low, you millions?

---

[102] Beethoven's rendition has been adopted as its anthem by the European Union after its formation in the 1970's.

Do you see your maker, world?
Search for Him above the stars,
Above the stars he must be living.
(translated from German by Michael Kay)

There is something exquisitely and achingly heart-wrenching about an isolated individual, cut off from contact with others by his disability, conceiving of a grand connectedness of humans and the cosmic forces ruling "above the stars". Beethoven, though, always transports us to emotions and experiences that go well beyond an expression in words.

Listening Experience 1: Beethoven Symphony no. 9 (conductor Wilhelm Furtwangler, Philharmonia Orchestra London, recorded at the Lucerne Festival, 1954).
https://www.youtube.com/watch?v=254ksoIiU_s
December 30, 2012. Accessed: 25.5.2021

Beethoven lived up to his commitment to universal brotherhood by including instruments from other parts of the world in this symphony, the Turkish bass drum and cymbals. He also stubbornly insisted on conducting the first performance in 1824, although the players followed their cue from another conductor; he could not hear the rapturous applause from the audience, so the players turned him around to view their enthusiastic response, and the acclaim continues two centuries later. Each of the four movements is a gem, but Furtwangler more than any other conductor seems to embody the aura of the slow third movement, where time seems suspended and the yearning for a new voice begins to take shape before emerging in the rapture of the "Ode to Joy".

Listening Experience 2: Brahms Symphony no. 1
(conductor Otto Klemperer, Philharmonia Orchestra; recorded 1956).
www.youtube.com/watch?v=HZkUkfJ8p4M&t=64s
February 28, 2013. Accessed: 26.5.2021

Johannes Brahms (1833-1897), like many composers in the 19th century, felt the weight of Beethoven's monumental oeuvre in attempting to establish their own inventive inspiration. It took him 43 years to complete his first symphony, and it was worth the preparation and anticipation, a work of panoramic and mature genius. From the ominous, thundering chords of the opening to the parting of the clouds in the last movement and the thrilling climax, this is the journey of a colossal triumph of the human spirit and mind over adversity. Brahms weaves in motifs and themes in enchanting variation and fulfilment, and the melody in the last movement bears the distinct imprint of Beethoven's "Ode to Joy". When the trumpets, horns, and trombones proclaim their exalted chorale in the coda, they propel the beautiful message to the heavens and above the stars, as Beethoven had envisioned.

Every listening of the Klemperer recording nourishes a catharsis with the perfect tempo. Brahms did indeed blaze Beethoven's torch with sounds most pleasing to the human ear and heart.

Sources/Citations

Amen, Daniel. *"11 risk factors that destroy your brain"*.
https://www.youtube.com/watch?v=AUBe5vkPPlY
January 11, 2019. Accessed: 20.8.2020

Bjorkman, Stig, Torsten Manns, Jonas Sima. 1973. *Bergman on Bergman.*
New York, Touchstone.

Eagleman, David. *"On Possibilianism".*
https://www.youtube.com/watch?v=lS0b4QCpFGc
December 1, 2010. Accessed: 6.5.2021

Goleman, Daniel. *Focus: the hidden driver of excellence"*. (Google Talks).
https://www.youtube.com/watch?v=b9yRmpcXKjY
December 6, 2013. Accessed: 8.9.2020

Kaku, Michio. *"Michio Kaku Explains String Theory"*.
https://www.youtube.com/watch?v=RZ5dj-Ozwm0&t=9s
November 12, 2013. Accessed: 15.5.2021

Kornfield, Jack. *"The Wisdom of Uncertainty"*.
www.youtube.com/watch?v=V3torYqRaOI&t=773s
July 7, 2017. Accessed:19.8.2020

McFarlane, Thomas J., ed. 2002. *Einstein and Buddha: The Parallel Sayings*. Berkeley, Ulysses Press.

Neuroplasticity with Professors David Eagleman and Andrew Huberman.
www.youtube.com/watch?v=zc_OXqCRL1g&t=454s
September 5, 2020. Accessed: 2.12.2020

Polk, Thad. *"Aging – it's not what you think"*.
https://www.youtube.com/watch?v=wrTISOuKg6o
April 20, 2016. Accessed: 29.8.2020

Revel, Jean-Francois and Matthieu Ricard. 1998. *The Monk and the Philosopher*. New York, Schocken Books.

Schaffner, Anna Katharina. *"You're not a computer, you're a tiny stone in a beautiful mosaic"*. Psyche (web): https://psyche.co. March 4, 2021

7 Habits of Happiness, with Dr. Daniel Amen.
https://www.youtube.com/watch?v=j6C9RJ0opxo
June 22, 2020. Accessed: 22.8.2020

Sinclair, David and Lewis Howes. *"Reverse your age today"*.
https://www.youtube.com/watch?v=8ZqAKNPxaxc
September 9, 2020. Accessed: 16.9.2020

St. Clair, Natalya. *"The Unexpected Math behind Van Gogh's Starry Night"*.
https://www.youtube.com/watch?v=PMerSm2ToFY
October 30, 2014. Accessed: 20.5.2021

TIFF 2020 (Toronto International Film Festival). *"Nomadland: Q&A with Chloe Zhao, Frances McDormand"*.
https://www.youtube.com/watch?v=Jc8X-6HI9d4&t=9s
September 13, 2020. Accessed: 8.5.2021

Times (The London Times). *"Gail Sheehy, Passages"*. September 4, 2020.

Trilling, Bernie and Fadel, Charles. 2009. *21st Century Skills – Learning for Life in Our Times.* San Francisco, Jossey-Bass/Wiley.

Vincent Van Gogh: Paintings, Drawings, Quotes, and Biography. Web: https://www.vincentvangogh.org/starry-night.jsp. Accessed: 22.5.2021

WEF (World Economic Forum): *"7 skills your child needs to survive the changing world of work"*. Web: www.weforum.org
September 4, 2017.

Wiegand, Chris. 2003. *Federico Fellini: The Complete Films.* Cologne, Taschen.

Wisden (Cricket Almanac). 1975. *"John Arlott: Sir Garfield Sobers - Cricket's Most Versatile Performer"*.

The Eighth Circle of Joy

After the exceptional outpouring of insight, wisdom, excellence, and synchrony in the seventh circle, it may strain our imagination to envisage a yet higher spring of inspirational vitality. Our intuitive passion, though, has reverberated with the aura of uplifting visions from sages, seers, prophets, poets, scientists and artists as a rapturous accompaniment in the human journey. Hovering above and encircling our being is the supreme energy of revelation.

We may begin to pierce the eternal mysteries of love, and its rippling diffusion from the womb to all forms of life and to our endangered planet. There is no greater urgency for our survival and flourishing than the restoration and empowering of the bonds of connectedness.

Poets and mystics discern truths that cleave our inner being. Scientists extend our lifespans and bring us closer to a throbbing cosmic music. Artists embellish our moments with images and sounds that propel instants of epiphany.

Beethoven gives voice to our gratitude for recovery and healing, which speaks directly to our time. Gratitude is the gateway to humility and abundance, the *Yinyang* of our joyful odyssey.

Radiating love: the vision of poets and mystics

The energy of love animates the universe, traversing the individual heart to humanity, embracing all forms of life and extending to exalted cosmic infinity. Yet, this ecstatic force also divides us in a dramatic dance of difference. We rely on poets and mystics to remind us of its elemental and healing power.

LOVE AFTER LOVE

by Derek Walcott[103]

The time will come
when, with elation,
you will greet yourself arriving
at your own door, in your own mirror,
and each will smile at the other's welcome,
and say, sit here. Eat.
You will love again the stranger who was your self.
Give wine. Give bread. Give back your heart
to itself, to the stranger who has loved you

all your life, whom you ignored
for another, who knows you by heart.
Take down the love letters from the bookshelf,

the photographs, the desperate notes,
peel your own image from the mirror.
Sit. Feast on your life.

Caribbean poet, Derek Walcott, celebrates the re-discovery of the self after the loss of a personal relationship. This is not a journey of the ego, rather a realization of the wellsprings of resilience and contentment that reside within our core. His metaphors of "eating" and "feasting" invite us to reclaim the appetite for living life at a tempo of our own making, the ingredients of delight imbibed in our wondrous journey.

---

[103] Source: Andrew Spacey, *Owlcation*. January 10,2020.

American poet, Maya Angelou, poses a more searching challenge and the possibility of a grander vision: could humans overcome their limited love for family, faith, and land; the tribal instincts that have torn us asunder in the past and continue to cast their ominous shadows today?

A BRAVE AND STARTLING TRUTH

by Maya Angelou[104]

We, this people, on a small and lonely planet
Traveling through casual space
Past aloof stars, across the way of indifferent suns
To a destination where all signs tell us
It is possible and imperative that we learn
A brave and startling truth

And when we come to it
To the day of peace making
When we release our fingers
From fists of hostility
And allow the pure air to cool our palms

When we come to it
When the curtain falls on the minstrel show of hate
And faces sooted with scorn are scrubbed clean
When battlefields and coliseum
No longer rake our unique and particular sons and daughters
Up with the bruised and bloody grass
To lie in identical plots in foreign soil

---

[104] Source: Maria Popova, *Brain Pickings*.

When the rapacious storming of the churches
The screaming racket in the temples have ceased
When the pennants are waving gaily
When the banners of the world tremble
Stoutly in the good, clean breeze

When we come to it
When we let the rifles fall from our shoulders
And children dress their dolls in flags of truce
When land mines of death have been removed
And the aged can walk into evenings of peace
When religious ritual is not perfumed
By the incense of burning flesh
And childhood dreams are not kicked awake
By nightmares of abuse

When we come to it
Then we will confess that not the Pyramids
With their stones set in mysterious perfection
Nor the Gardens of Babylon
Hanging as eternal beauty
In our collective memory
Not the Grand Canyon
Kindled into delicious colour
By Western sunsets

Nor the Danube, flowing its blue soul into Europe
Not the sacred peak of Mount Fuji
Stretching to the Rising Sun
Neither Father Amazon nor Mother Mississippi who, without favour,
Nurture all creatures in the depths and on the shores
These are not the only wonders of the world

When we come to it
We, this people, on this minuscule and kithless globe
Who reach daily for the bomb, the blade and the dagger
Yet who petition in the dark for tokens of peace
We, this people on this mote of matter
In whose mouths abide cankerous words
Which challenge our very existence
Yet out of those same mouths
Come songs of such exquisite sweetness
That the heart falters in its labour
And the body is quieted into awe

We, this people, on this small and drifting planet
Whose hands can strike with such abandon
That in a twinkling, life is sapped from the living
Yet those same hands can touch with such healing, irresistible tenderness
That the haughty neck is happy to bow
And the proud back is glad to bend
Out of such chaos, of such contradiction
We learn that we are neither devils nor divines

When we come to it
We, this people, on this wayward, floating body
Created on this earth, of this earth
Have the power to fashion for this earth
A climate where every man and every woman
Can live freely without sanctimonious piety
Without crippling fear

When we come to it
We must confess that we are the possible
We are the miraculous, the true wonder of this world
That is when, and only when
We come to it.

"We learn that we are neither devils nor divines". Could humans live with this piercingly candid admission of imperfection, in ourselves and in others, so that we create harmony in what the astronomer, Carl Sagan, called "our little blue dot"?[105]

The grand civilizations of India and Persia germinated traditions of spiritual seekers and mystics who galvanized the yearning for unity that Angelou voiced in our time. The wandering mentor, Guru Nanak, birthed Sikhism, a faith renowned for removing social distinctions and selfless service to others:

> He who regards all men as equals is religious.
> If the people use the wealth bestowed on them by God for
> themselves alone or for treasuring it, it is like a corpse. But if
> they decide to share it with others, it becomes sacred food. (Nanak).

Both Nanak and the Indian mystic Kabir cautioned us five centuries ago that human concerns had to be surpassed in our love for nature and the planet, a message with a poignant resonance in our current reality:

> What should the yogi have to fear?
> Trees, plants, and all
> that is inside and outside,
> is He Himself.
> (Nanak)[106]
>
> Everyone talks of compassion,
> None knows its essence
> One who has no love for all creatures,

---

[105] Sagan referred to the photograph of Earth taken by the Voyager 1 spacecraft in 1990, and its image of a tiny world, for him, underscored the responsibility to "deal more kindly with one another and to cherish the pale blue dot".

[106] Source: https://quotes.thefamouspeople.com/guru-nanak-3656.php. Accessed: 30.5.2021

How can he possess kindness?[107]
(Kabir)

The Buddhist poet and spiritual leader, Thich Nhat Hanh, amplifies the message of the Buddha on "true love"[108], a blend of four elements: "*maitri*" or loving-kindness, the capacity to offer happiness to others; "*karuna*" or compassion, the energy that can help remove suffering in the self and the other person; radiating joy; and inclusiveness, which removes any separation or frontier between us and all existence. The Buddha's unbounded love in the "*Sutta Nipata*" brings together the inspirations of Wolcott, Angelou, Nanak and Kabir, beginning with our most beautiful initiation into the world:

Just as a mother with her own life
Protects her child, her only child, from harm,
So within yourself let grow
A boundless love for all creatures.
Let your love flow outward through the universe,
To its height, its depth, its broad extent,
A limitless love, without hatred or enmity.
Then, as you stand or walk,
Sit or lie down,
As long as you are awake,
Strive for this with a one-pointed mind:
Your life will bring heaven to earth.

The Persian Sufi[109] poet, Rumi, offers a yearning for love that could only arise from a shattering of the veils of partition and division that propel the mystic's boon and shared enrapture:

---

[107] Source: G.N. Das. 1999. *The Maxims of Kabir*. New Delhi, Abhinav Publications.
[108] Source: Thich Nhat Hanh, *True Love*. https://www.youtube.com/watch?v=hDbj-Y9w8KU, January 9 2020. Accessed: 29.5.2021
[109] Sufis or "people of wool" are ascetics and mystics in the Islamic faith.

I want that love that moved the mountains.
I want that love that split the ocean.
I want that love that made the winds tremble.
I want that love that roared like thunder.
I want that love that will raise the dead.
I want that love that lifts us to ecstasy.
I want that love that is the silence of eternity[110].

Rumi has released the primordial spark that abides in the depths of our being. The fire of union and fulfilment encompasses all moments of creation, daring to defy dissolution. Silence, though, carries its own potent impulse- and yet, a vibrating presence endures. Music and silence must continue as inseparable companions.

Where Everything Is Music

by Rumi

Don't worry about saving these songs!
And if one of our instruments breaks,
it doesn't matter.
We have fallen into the place
where everything is music.
The strumming and the flute notes
rise into the atmosphere,
and even if the whole world's harp
should burn up, there will still be
hidden instruments playing.
So the candle flickers and goes out.
We have a piece of flint, and a spark.
This singing art is sea foam.
The graceful movements come from a pearl

---

[110] Source: *relicsworld.com* (accessed: 20.5.2021)

somewhere on the ocean floor.
Poems reach up like spindrift and the edge
of driftwood along the beach, wanting!
They derive
from a slow and powerful root
that we can't see.
Stop the words now.
Open the window in the centre of your chest,
and let the spirits fly in and out[111].

Music beats in every human breast, in every living creature, in the cosmic sphere. Occasionally, a mind comes along which miraculously spans the space between our inner song and the celestial melody. Beethoven achieved this in his late string quartets, while continuing a struggle with deafness and physical ailments. Each of the quartets mingles the intimacy of a conversation with adventurous explorations of a journey into previously unknown terrain. In the third movement of the string quartet no. 15, Beethoven expressed his gratitude for recovery from an illness, using the Lydian mode, which is historically associated with healing and recovery. He included the title for this movement, *"A Convalescent's Holy Song of Thanksgiving"*.

Listening Experience: Beethoven String Quartet no. 15, op. 132, third movement. Emerson String Quartet.
https://www.youtube.com/watch?v=6rCapLO-6eU
November 10, 2018. Accessed: 29.5.2021

We can relate acutely to this music in our experience with the Covid pandemic and our hope for recovery and restoration of health. Beethoven,

---

[111] Source: *relicsworld.com* (accessed 20.5.2021). The best source for the poems of Rumi are the translations by Coleman Barks.

though, elevates the sound to a universal and eternal magnitude and intensity, a promise that our planet may yet rediscover the voice of healing.

It is difficult to conceive of anything more profound in the human experience than these hypnotic eighteen minutes, as we extend to the edge of consciousness.

Silence alone must follow.